GW00708201

Freelancing

Ros Jay

TEACH YOURSELF BOOKS

Order queries: please contact Bookpoint Ltd, 39 Milton Park, Abingdon, Oxon OX14 4TD. Telephone: (44) 01235 400414, Fax: (44) 01235 400454. Lines are open from 9.00–6.00, Monday to Saturday, with a 24 hour message answering service. Email address: orders@bookpoint.co.uk

British Library Cataloguing in Publication Data
A catalogue entry for this title is available from The British Library.

ISBN 0 340 72121 9

First published 1998
Impression number   10 9 8 7 6 5 4 3 2 1
Year   2002 2001 2000 1999 1998

The 'Teach Yourself' name and logo are registered trade marks of Hodder & Stoughton Ltd.

Copyright © 1998 Ros Jay

All rights reserved. No part of this publication may be reproduced or transmitted in any form or by any means, electronic or mechanical, including photocopy, recording, or any information storage and retrieval system, without permission in writing from the publisher or under licence from the Copyright Licensing Agency Limited. Further details of such licences (for reprographic reproduction) may be obtained from the Copyright Licensing Agency Limited, of 90 Tottenham Court Road, London W1P 9HE.

Typeset by Transet Limited, Coventry, England.
Printed in Great Britain for Hodder & Stoughton Educational, a division of Hodder Headline Plc, 338 Euston Road, London NW1 3BH by Cox & Wyman Ltd, Reading, Berkshire.

CONTENTS

INTRODUCTION

The idea of being a freelance appeals to most of us. As a freelance you probably work from home – often *at* home; you can broadly speaking choose your own hours; you're your own boss. All you need is a skill you can sell and hey presto! you're off and running.

But it isn't really quite that simple. Yes, it does have lots of advantages. And yes, it works very well for a lot of people. But you need many more skills than the one you're selling. Suppose you're a personnel manager and you've decided to go freelance as a consultant. Or you used to be an accountant, and now the kids have gone back to school you want to set up as a freelance doing other people's book-keeping for them. Or perhaps you're a journalist on a local paper and you want to freelance for several newspapers and magazines.

Obviously you need to understand personnel issues, know how to keep accounts, or be a good writer with an eye for a promising story. But there are several other skills you will need no matter which of these professions you choose to freelance in.

Having what it takes

First of all, before you even begin to earn, you need to have – or learn – the right temperament to freelance. If you have no self-discipline and cannot get out of bed in the morning you cannot be a successful freelance. If you can't keep the kids out of your study you will have problems earning a living. If you cannot cope emotionally with financial insecurity or with rejection, you will find freelancing a great strain.

Once you have decided you have (or can acquire) the necessary characteristics, you need to set yourself up with the equipment you will need and with a space to put it in. And you will need to square things with your bank manager, and probably find yourself an accountant and perhaps a solicitor.

You've got your equipment, your office and the professional advice you need. Now you need to learn to manage your time effectively. That means not only doing the job your clients pay you for, but also finding time to do the books, tout for new work, respond to phone calls and messages, send out invoices and fill in your tax return. And maybe – if you're really organised – even go on holiday occasionally. Fitting home life around work is one of the things many freelances find hardest of all.

Setting up

What are you going to charge for your services? Too little, and you can't make a living. Too much, and you won't get any clients – you still can't make a living. Negotiating fees is one of the most important skills any freelance must acquire. It ties in with another important skill: getting the right level of work. The odds on your clients collectively requiring exactly 40 hours' work a week from you, every week, are not great. What will you do if you're lucky enough to be in demand 110 hours a week?

And once you have made all these decisions, you will have to organise yourself a book-keeping system and then sort out your invoicing, tax and possibly VAT. You may also need a pension, insurance and other financial arrangements.

Finding the work

You're ready to go. You've got all your equipment and systems in place, and you know what you're charging and how you will respond if you are offered more work than you can handle. Even the tax man is happy. Now all you need to do is find some work.

This obviously calls for a crucial set of skills. If you don't master the basic techniques of selling you're going to be in trouble, no matter how useful a skill you have to offer. As a freelance, you are essentially selling yourself, so the way you come across is vitally important. From good time-keeping to well-presented letters, your image must be professional.

Freelances often have to sell themselves through sales proposals or by giving a sales presentation to prospects. Again, these are important skills to learn in order to be sure that you don't miss out on work. After all, as a freelance, the link between getting the work and paying the bills is more nerve-wrackingly obvious than it is as an employee. Working for someone else, a lost contract may not make any difference to your pay packet.

Working for yourself, a lost contract can mean at best cancelling this year's holiday; at worst, cancelling tonight's supper.

Teach Yourself Freelancing is all about mastering this portfolio of skills which you need in order to succeed as a freelance. Armed with the information here, you should be able to set yourself up, organise your work and recruit and retain good clients. Then you can concentrate on the skill you are selling – consultancy, book-keeping, journalism or whatever else – knowing that if anyone can make a good living at it, you can.

Part One
DECIDING TO GO FREELANCE

1 | WHAT IS A FREELANCE?

In order to become a freelance, you need to know what it means. In medieval times, a freelance was precisely that: a free lance – a mercenary soldier who came with his own weapon, whose services could be bought for a limited period, after which he would be free to go and fight on someone else's behalf.

Things haven't changed that much, except that most freelances nowadays aren't expected to kill anyone. But as a freelance you work for several clients who are buying your personal time; they are not paying for just anyone to do the work. If you hired the best mercenary soldier in the land for a particularly nasty skirmish, and he sent along a young apprentice on his first assignment, you wouldn't be pleased. In the same way, if someone employs you as a freelance to do their gardening, they don't want some other gardener turning up who may not know a dahlia from a daisy. It is your personal skill which clients will buy.

Freelances sell a skill, which means that they sell a service and not a product. You may need equipment to do the job, in which case you will provide it; if you are a freelance mural painter you will use your own paints and brushes. If you are a PR you might write a press release for a client and supply it printed on a sheet of paper, but the client is not buying the piece of paper, they are buying the skilful writing you have printed on it.

Classic freelancing style

There are many characteristics typical to freelancing, although not every freelance has every characteristic. But typically, a freelance has clients and not customers – people (who may or may not represent an organisation) with whom you have an ongoing relationship. The work you do tends to mean that you have a few clients to whom you sell large chunks of your time, rather than lots of little clients. And you are responsible for finding these clients for yourself by advertising, word of mouth or whatever means you choose.

Negotiating fees

Your clients negotiate a fee with you; you may have a fixed rate or you may not. Either way, it is unlikely that you will publish it – you won't offer prospects a catalogue and price list. The client will ask 'What will you charge?' For many freelances, this leads to a negotiation because you can offer different levels of service depending on what they are prepared to pay.

Some clients will offer you a retainer for your services for a regular number of hours a week or a month. But many freelances do not negotiate on the basis of the number of hours they work at all. They agree a fair fee for the work, and so long as they deliver on time and to standard it is no concern of the client's how long it takes them. The client is buying their skill, not their time.

Working from home

As a freelance, you probably work from home. You may not work *at* home all the time because you may visit your clients' premises to work, but you will generally be based at home. That will be your postal address, your phone location (other than a mobile); it will be where your fax machine, your computer, your record books and so on are kept. When you take time out from earning in order to do your paperwork, you'll probably do it in a study at home (or on the kitchen table, or in the spare bedroom).

Some freelances work from a studio or office away from home. This is usually either a small rented single room which they rent because there is no convenient space in the house, or a studio they use because their work demands a specialised space. If, for example, you are a portrait painter you will need the kind of studio which most homes can't provide.

Neither employer nor employee

The word freelance has no legal standing. Freelances are, technically, self-employed. They pay their own tax and their own National Insurance contribution. You are not an employee because the clients who buy your services do not deduct any money from you for such purposes. Nor do they have any legal obligation to pay you sick pay, maternity allowance or any other employee benefits, even if they have paid you a retainer for several years. They do not make payments to you automatically on their payroll; you invoice them for services rendered.

It is important to know whether you are technically employed or freelance, because it is a topic the Inland Revenue feel strongly about. They do not appreciate people who they consider to be employees claiming to be freelances. If you make an arrangement with your employer that you will continue to do exactly the job you do now, under the same conditions, except that you will come off the payroll and start invoicing for your work, the tax people are almost bound to consider that you are still an employee.

There is no specific formula for defining whether you are employed or self-employed, since the Inland Revenue judge each case on its own merits. However, the following list tells you the main criteria the tax people will use for assessing your status.

- ■ *How many companies are you working for?* If you have several clients you are almost certainly self-employed (but you could have several part-time jobs). If you have only one client, it gets harder – though not impossible – to convince the tax people you are not an employee.

- ■ *What happens if you are sick or go on holiday?* The idea here is that an employee is paid for time off for sickness or holiday, and a self-employed person is not.

- ■ *Who fixes your hours of work?* Can you claim overtime? Once again, an employee is generally told how many hours to work and when, and is paid on an hourly, weekly or monthly basis. As a freelance, you probably set your own hours and are usually paid a fee for the work regardless of how long it takes.

- ■ *Do you have your own office provided for your use?* A self-employed person probably doesn't work at the client's premises (although some may do, such as computer programmers). If you have your own office in your client's premises, with your name on the door, it will take a lot to persuade the Revenue that you are not an employee.

- ■ *Are you on an internal phone list? Does the company you work for give you a business card with their logo on it?* Both of these would make it very difficult to argue that you are self-employed.

- *Who provides the tools and equipment to do the job?* An employer generally provides the basic equipment such as a computer, fax machine, car, drawing board or whatever you need. If you provide your own this supports the case that you are self-employed.

- *If your work is not satisfactory, who bears the cost?* Can the client refuse to pay you if your work doesn't meet the agreed standard? If it has to be redone, do you have to do it in your own time? If so, you are probably self-employed. If, however, your employer would call you in for a dressing down but your pay packet would come through anyway, you are most likely an employee.

This list is not exhaustive; if you are still unsure you can ask advice at your Social Security Office. The key thing the Inland Revenue want to establish is whether you are under the control of the company or organisation in question. If they think you are, you will be classed as an employee.

Bear in mind that it is possible to be both employed in a part-time job and working as a freelance in your remaining time. In this case, the Inland Revenue will treat each situation separately for tax purposes.

Technically, you can employ other people if you are self-employed by applying to open a payroll. However, the term freelance is not generally applied to someone who is operating in this way, and for the purposes of this book we will assume that you are not an employer. If you have more work than you can handle you might pass it on to someone else, possibly taking a cut (as we shall see in Chapter 7), but as a freelance you would do this in a way which does not constitute employing them.

Not only do freelances (in the generally accepted sense of the word) not employ anyone else; they also have very few suppliers. You probably have a stationery supplier, and someone you buy computer consumables from, but these are for your own administration. If you are a painter you will need to buy brushes and canvases and a few other basics. But a freelance doesn't sell a product, and consequently you don't have to buy in raw materials.

Are you a freelance?

If you want to know whether what you do, or plan to do, is freelancing in the sense which this book is designed to cover, have a look through the checklist in Figure 1.1. For each pair of statements tick one or other column.

1 I regard the people I work for as . . .	clients ☐	customers ☐
2 I have . . .	a few main clients ☐	lots of small customers ☐
3 I am paid a . . .	negotiable fee ☐	fixed hourly/daily/ weekly rate ☐
4 If I am ill or on holiday . . .	I don't get paid ☐	I get paid anyway ☐
5 If my work is not up to standard . . .	I don't get paid ☐	I get paid anyway ☐
6 My clients expect the work to be done by . . .	me ☐	either me or someone I contract to do it ☐
7 I am selling . . .	a service ☐	a product ☐
8 I do the work . . .	after agreement with the client ☐	and then try to find someone to buy it ☐
9 The equipment I use is . . .	my own ☐	supplied by the client ☐
10 I have . . .	few suppliers ☐	a lot of regular suppliers ☐
11 I work . . .	from, if not at, home ☐	from outside the home ☐
12 My business card carries . . .	my own logo ☐	someone else's logo ☐
13 I employ . . .	no one ☐	one or more people ☐
14 My tax and NIC are paid . . .	by me ☐	by someone other than me ☐

Figure 1.1 Checklist to determine freelance status

If all or almost all your options fall in the left-hand column, you are a freelance. If a lot of them fall in the right-hand column, you probably aren't. If you have ticked the right-hand column for the final statement, you are definitely not a freelance.

Freelance options

That's a fairly full description of what being a freelance – as opposed to anything else – entails. But what do freelances actually do? If you fancy the idea of being freelance but aren't sure what skill to sell, what are your options? Here are some examples of jobs which are freelance in nature, or which can be done on a freelance basis:

- writer
- designer
- consultant
- illustrator
- journalist
- book-keeper
- computer programmer
- make-up artist

- researcher
- PR
- trainer
- painter
- software engineer
- actor
- gardener
- media buyer

It can't be emphasised too strongly that going freelance is like setting out in any other form of self-employment or small business. If there isn't a ready market for what you do, you won't make a living at it. As with any other line of business, you need to do your research thoroughly before you begin to make sure you aren't pinning your livelihood on a doomed venture. Chapter 9 looks at how to find work as a freelance; if you sound out potential clients before you give up your current job you can get a picture of whether you are likely to drum up enough work to make it worthwhile.

The most popular approach is to find a handful of potential clients, often including your current employer, who say that they will buy your services if you become a freelance. Mind you, be warned that the proportion who do what they say they will is always a lot lower than you hoped.

Freelancing does have lots of advantages over employment, but it is also hard work, and you become responsible for a lot of things an employer has previously looked after for you. These can include finding clients, cultivating and maintaining a good relationship with them, handling invoicing, book-keeping and other administrative tasks, paying your tax and NIC, providing office or studio space, paying phone bills and other overheads, setting your salary, and making sure there is money in your pay packet at the end of the month.

Summary

- Typically, a freelance has clients not customers. The freelance sells a skill, and so provides a service, not a product.
- A freelance is neither an employer nor an employee. Freelances often work from home and are responsible for negotiating their own fees.
- Work through the checklist in Figure 1.1 to determine whether you are a freelance.

2 | IS FREELANCING FOR YOU?

Some people find freelancing very easy and rewarding, while others find it hard work for all the wrong reasons. Not only do you need to be skilled in your particular line of work, and able to sell yourself effectively; you also need to have the right temperament for freelancing. For many people, the reality of freelancing is far less enjoyable than the idea.

Emotional support

If you are switching to freelancing from a very different lifestyle, it can involve a lot of changes. Many of these can be quite difficult to cope with until you get used to them, such as cash flow problems, handling rejection, new working hours and so on. Most people find they need support from friends or family to help them through the transition period – and often beyond.

Knowing other freelances is a big help, too, as they are a terrific source of advice. Even experienced freelances call each other up for advice, such as 'You do more of this sort of work than I do. What would you charge?' Or 'I've got a bad feeling about this client – tell me what you think.' There's no doubt that you are at a big advantage if you can talk to other people in the same boat.

If you are involved in a relationship, especially if you are living with a partner, your switch to freelancing will inevitably affect him or her. You will almost certainly find yourself wanting or needing to work at least some evenings and weekends. Will your partner support you? Put up with it? Leave you? (One woman, whose husband left his job to become a freelance, objected 'I married him for better or for worse, but not for lunch.')

If your finances are interlinked, your increase – or drop – in income will affect your partner. Is your partner prepared for this? How would your partner react to being told that your income is half what it was last year? Will your partner mind giving up this year's holiday, or taking the kids out of private education?

Some people can manage with little emotional support in times of change, while others need a lot. Which are you? If you are in a long-term relationship, your partner's support – even when things go wrong – is essential. Freelancing can break up relationships.

Working alone

Most freelance jobs, though not all, involve spending a lot of time working alone. Since you have neither an employer nor any employees, nor a business partner, you necessarily have no colleagues. The only human contact you are likely to have is with your clients. Usually this amounts to no more than a few phone calls a day unless you happen to be, say, a freelance make-up artist.

Some people who work in busy offices long for peace and quiet, while others find the bustle and the company of their colleagues motivating. Some think they want peace and quiet but, when they achieve it, find they don't really like it as much as they thought. After the first hour or two they begin to miss the activity.

For some people, the appeal of employment is not to do with the socialising or the air of activity, but with the need to be part of a structured hierarchy. Some of us like to be part of a social group and to know our position in it. If you are a pack animal, you may feel lost working for yourself.

If you work with other people and are thinking of going freelance in a fairly solitary profession, try spending a few days monitoring your contact with other people to see how it affects you. Does it irritate you, or do you enjoy the social interaction? Does it interfere with your productivity? Do you find it easier to develop ideas by bouncing them off other people? Do you look forward to periods of isolation, or to periods of social contact?

Some of us enjoy meetings, while others prefer to take tasks away from the meeting and work on them alone. Are you happier disappearing on your own with a bundle of papers and converting them into a report, or sitting in a meeting threshing out the issues with your colleagues? By focusing on how you feel about working around other people while you're actually doing it, you should get a clearer picture of how you would cope working on your own.

Getting motivated

As a freelance, you generally don't get paid until the job is completed. If you are one of those people who never completes anything, you will never earn any money. Do you find it easy to get out of bed in the mornings? Once up, do you get on with the jobs which need doing, or do you mess about rereading your post and making cups of coffee?

As well as the issue of being motivated to work in general, how good are you at motivating yourself to do specific tasks – the boring ones, the difficult ones, the ones you don't like, the ones with no deadline and so on? Presumably you would be unlikely to freelance doing a job you hated, but even if you love writing, illustrating or playing with computers, there's more to freelancing than that – which is what this book is all about.

For example, you have to be able to sell yourself to drum up future business – how good are you at motivating yourself to do that? Even the most straightforward freelance job has a certain amount of financial administration attached to it. Will you get round to keeping your accounts, organising your invoices, filling in your tax return and keeping on top of your correspondence?

Some freelances find their motivation is influenced by professional pride – they cannot bring themselves to do work they see as demeaning. Unless you are very lucky, however, you will probably have to take any work you can get when you set out. If you are only prepared to do the prestige work, and can't find it in you to do more basic work, you could have problems. Perhaps you want to go freelance as a journalist specialising in countryside matters. You probably prefer to work for national magazines and newspapers, but you may find that you can't make a living unless you also take work from local papers and small-circulation, non-specialist magazines.

You don't have to be the most motivated person in the world in order to be freelance, but you do need to be able to motivate yourself sufficiently to do the job. If you don't have to work specific hours you may get away with staying in bed until 10 o'clock most mornings, so long as you work well once you're up, and work until seven in the evening if you need to.

You may not be able to keep on top of your accounts all the time, but so long as you can make yourself organise them and bring them up to date once every couple of months, that may be enough. You don't have to be superhuman, but do be realistic. If you are one of those people who needs someone standing over them, nagging them or enthusing them in order to work you're not alone. But think twice before you go freelance, or you may find you can't earn enough to live on.

Organising your time

Chapter 5 is all about how to manage your time, so I shan't go into the details here. The relevant question at this stage is, quite simply, can you do it? You don't have to be the most organised person in the world, but you have to be able to achieve and maintain a certain level of order.

If business goes well, you will find your time is pretty full. When this happens, the difference between good and bad time management can be measured in hard cash. If you are unorganised you will not be able to take on and fit in as much work as you would if you were well organised. In the worst case, you will lose clients through not completing work on time because you hadn't scheduled it properly. The ability to meet deadlines is essential as a freelance.

With several clients, you have a particular problem – you have to fit them all round each other. And you have to do it without putting any of their noses out of joint. Good time management is essential as a freelance. I'm not suggesting that you shouldn't go freelance unless you are already highly organised. You simply have to be confident that you can learn the necessary skills, at least to a level where your work doesn't suffer from poor time management.

Finding some peace and quiet

Almost all freelances start off based at home, even if they later decide to rent an office somewhere. That means you have to be able to achieve an atmosphere in which you can work properly. If you have an open plan house and several noisy children, this can be difficult.

You need to be certain that you will be able to work in peace when you need to. Either you need a space which is set apart from the rest of the household, or you need enough regular time when everyone else is out of the house. If the children are at school and your partner works full time you will have several hours of peace between the periods of pandemonium, and this might be enough. If you live alone, congratulations – you have it made.

Of course, some people can only work in total silence, while others can manage fine even in the middle of a battle zone. Which are you? The next chapter will look in more detail at how to achieve the level of isolation you need.

Handling the knock-backs

As a freelance you will have to tout for business yourself. And, as with any business, not every prospect will become a client – some will turn you down. Some people are very philosophical about this; they expect it and aren't in the least upset when it happens. Others find it demoralising and hard to deal with.

It is made worse as a freelance because you are essentially selling yourself. You're not asking prospects if they would like a personnel consultant, for example; you're asking them if they would like *you* as a personnel consultant. This makes any rejection feel far more personal. Since the key to handling rejection is not to take it personally, you can see how much harder this becomes if you are freelance.

In fact, few prospects are cruel enough to be personal about rejection. They probably genuinely didn't want a personnel consultant at all, or thought you were great but too expensive, or so much in demand you wouldn't be able to give them enough time. But what they intend and what you feel do not always tally. Most freelances start out finding rejection unpleasant, and gradually learn to brush it off. If you find it hard but manageable, you'll probably learn to cope fine.

But don't delude yourself. Handling rejection well is a big part of being freelance. If you are going to become demoralised and depressed – and plenty of people understandably do – you should consider seriously whether freelancing is really for you. We'll look at how to cope with knock-backs in more detail in Chapter 9.

Living without security

The traditional 'job for life' barely exists any longer. Even so, being employed gives you far more security than being freelance. In fact, anything gives you more security than being freelance. As an employee, broadly speaking, you cannot be sacked without good reason, you may well be part of a company pension scheme, if you're made redundant you'll get redundancy pay – and if you lose your job you may well get another one doing the same thing for someone else.

What's more, you know what your earnings will be this month, this year and next year. They may go up, but they are unlikely to go down. This makes it far easier to budget for living expenses, holidays, the mortgage, school fees and any other regular expenses.

As a freelance, on the other hand, you can almost never predict your earnings either accurately or very far ahead. If you're lucky you will have some short-term guaranteed earnings. You may have a fixed-term contract with a client – but what will you do if it isn't renewed? You may have royalties if you're a writer, or perhaps if you're an illustrator – but how long will they keep coming in for?

You will, however, have no shortage of guaranteed outgoings. Household bills, tax bills, mortgage repayments and so on. There are few freelances alive who haven't suffered some sleepless nights worrying whether their earnings will cover their outgoings. But if you are the type to lose sleep every night over it, even if the figures are adding up satisfactorily for the moment, you may well find that freelancing just isn't worth the worry.

Limited earnings

From the financial point of view, freelances usually have another restriction. There tends to be a maximum amount you can earn, because you are selling your own time and you have only a limited amount of it. If you were a manufacturer and you sold an average of a hundred items a week, someone might put in a regular order for five hundred items a week, and your profits would jump. But as a freelance, if someone wants to offer you fifty hours' work a week and you're already working full time, you simply can't take the work (unless you want to move into running a business rather than freelancing).

So if you work forty hours a week, and your hourly rate is £10, it doesn't take much to see that you simply aren't going to earn more than £400 a week. That may not sound too bad, but take out time for holidays, illness, doing your accounts and chasing jobs which come to nothing (we'll look at this in more detail in Chapter 6), and you've got a relatively modest income which you have no scope for exceeding. Some freelances may charge £50 an hour, or £100, but they still have a maximum earning potential that wouldn't exist if they started a business and took on extra staff to cope with an increase in workload.

There are a few freelance jobs which have a potential for extra earnings, such as writing (where you can earn royalties), but most do not. This, you might say, is no different from working for an employer where your salary is fixed. However, when you are employed, your salary is not only your maximum but also your minimum income. As a freelance, on the other hand, there is no minimum income – except unemployment benefit.

Are you the freelancing type?

That's an overview of the most typical problems people encounter as freelances from the point of view of temperament. Of course even the most successful freelances find some bits tougher than others. You don't have to be perfect at everything. But it is important, before you launch into a freelance career, to be confident that you won't find yourself miserable and penniless simply because you're not cut out for the lifestyle.

Figure 2.1 is a self-assessment questionnaire for you to answer, to help give you an idea of how well suited you are to the freelance life. Do answer it honestly or it won't help you (you can always revise your scores upwards later to impress anyone else who borrows this book). For each of the statements, rate yourself on a scale of nought to five (where nought is 'I am utterly hopeless in this department' and five is 'I could do it with my eyes shut'). When you reach the end, add up your total score.

Now see how well suited you are to freelancing by reading the assessments below.

■ **Score 40–50**: What are you waiting for? It sounds as though you'll thoroughly enjoy freelancing, and be very good at it. So long as you have a saleable skill you won't go far wrong.

■ **Score 30–39**: You may have to make an effort to learn some of the skills you need to freelance, but it shouldn't be beyond

Statement	0	1	2	3	4	5	
I have all the emotional support I need							
I work happily and productively on my own							
I am self-disciplined about meeting deadlines							
I am good at getting on with tasks I don't enjoy							
I am good at organising my time							
I can work effectively despite some noise and interruptions							
I have a philosophical attitude to rejection							
I am good at selling myself							
I don't need financial security in order to be happy							
I don't mind if my earnings cannot rise above a certain level							
Total							

Figure 2.1 Self-assessment questionnaire to determine suitability for freelancing

you to grasp them. While freelancing may not come entirely naturally to you, you should find that once you are into the swing of it you find the lifestyle relatively easy.

■ **Score 20–29**: You're not a classic freelance type, and you need to consider hard whether it would really be a sensible move. However, if you scored worst in areas which are least relevant to your particular line of work, and are good at learning new skills (the ones this book is all about), you may succeed.

■ **Score 10–19**: It's very unlikely that you would be happy or successful freelancing, even though the idea of working for yourself may appeal to you. If you really can't resist trying it, make sure you have some other form of income as well such as a part-time job which you fit your freelance work around.

■ **Score 0–10**: Don't give up the day job. Seriously. Freelance if you must, but don't expect too much, and don't rely on it as a source of income.

If you scored either 1 or 2 for any statement, even if your overall score was high, you should look very carefully at the poor scoring areas. If you score only 1 for coping with rejection, for example, freelancing may not be for you even if you are ideally suited in every other respect. However, you may feel that you could learn to improve in your weakest areas. Or, if you're lucky, you may be planning to freelance in an area where you don't need this particular skill – if you're setting up as a freelance while maintaining a separate regular income, the financial insecurity probably doesn't matter to you.

This chapter and Chapter 1 have looked at what a freelance is and whether you want to be one. By now, you should have a clearer idea about the answers to these questions. Now it's time to look at how to set yourself up and get the help you need.

Summary

- As a freelance, you need to be able to cope with the following: the need to have emotional support; working alone; getting motivated; being able to organise your time; finding some peace and quiet in order to work; being able to handle the knock-backs; living without security and living on limited earnings.

- Find out if you are suited to dealing with the problems faced by freelances by completing the self-assessment questionnaire in Figure 2.1.

3 | SETTING UP

Before you start to invite work, you will need to set yourself up with a space to work from and some basic equipment. Start-up costs for freelancing tend to be relatively low, and can be offset against tax (see Chapter 8), but you will need at least a few basics.

Where should you be?

Location

You have to work from a base somewhere, even if all your earning time is spent on your clients' premises, because you still have to have somewhere to sit and do your planning, your accounts and so on. Most freelances choose to work from home for reasons which are probably obvious: it's cheaper, it already has a lot of the facilities you want (phone, heating, chairs, kettle and so on), and it makes getting to work in the morning very easy. However, sometimes it may make sense to work from a base away from home.

Working from home

This is by far the most popular freelancing option, but one which can require quite a lot of effort in terms of upheaval, discipline and a change in attitude from everyone in the house.

The first thing you need is somewhere you can use. Many people use the kitchen table, the spare bedroom or the garage. When I first started freelancing I worked in a cupboard on the landing with the double doors taken off. I even know someone who ingeniously converted the downstairs lavatory into a study. A cupboard above the loo had a door hinged at the bottom which folded down to form a desk supported on the cistern. He sat astride the toilet to use the desk. (If you're looking for a low budget study, I guess that's one way to avoid spending too many pennies.)

We'll look at the amount of space you need in a moment; but the first thing is to make sure you have a workable location. For one thing, you need to make sure that you have access to all the services you need. In particular, you are going to need an electricity supply, for light, heating and equipment, and a phone line (almost certainly). It's no good deciding to work from a room such as a garage which doesn't have these facilities, if you can't afford to install them.

Having made sure you have everything you need, the next thing is to make sure you can eliminate what you don't need – in particular noise and interruptions. If you live alone it's probably fairly simple (unless you have a cat and are trying to work on the kitchen table – a clean sheet of paper is a magnet to a cat with muddy paws). If there are other people in the house or flat, it can be harder unless they are out all day.

Flatmates and housemates can usually be persuaded to keep out of your way, so long as you haven't taken over the kitchen (or the loo). A partner can be harder to control for some reason, but it has to be done. If your partner managed without you when you were at work, the same should still apply even when you happen to be upstairs. If your partner, or a childminder, is responsible for keeping small children out of your way, things get even more interesting.

There are two points to establish firmly in these situations. The first is that if you cannot achieve the level of peace and quiet you need to work productively, you will have to give up freelancing, or rent an office elsewhere – an expense which will cut the family income. This usually gives a partner the incentive to co-operate.

The second point is to ask that the partner or childminder applies the same principles for interrupting you as they would if you were working in an office. If an emergency would have justified calling you at work, it justifies interrupting you at home – but not otherwise.

You may, depending on your work and your style of working, alleviate the situation further by having certain times of day when you emerge from isolation and are available for conversation. Perhaps you come out to make yourself coffee or tea mid-morning and mid-afternoon. And you could take a lunch break which you share with the family. For many people, these are among the perks that give freelancing its appeal. If this is the case, do it – just make sure you don't fritter away too much time.

One other thing can help, too. If you have two phone lines, with extensions in your study as well as elsewhere in the house, your partner can use one of them to call you up on the other line. This might sound daft, and it certainly isn't the cheapest form of communication when you're both in the same house already (unless you have two extensions on the same line with an intercom facility), but it does have its advantages. For one thing, phone interruptions are usually less distracting than personal visits; you can even leave the phone unanswered if you're concentrating particularly hard on something. And for another thing, a phone conversation is likely to be quicker.

One final word of warning, which just about anyone who works from home will confirm. Most people who have never freelanced seem to think that working from home isn't a real job. Consequently you will find that just when you are stuck into a task which demands particular concentration, your mum rings for a chat, or one of your mates calls to ask if you fancy going for a drink on Friday night – calls they would never have made when you worked for someone else in an office.

Convincing these people that you really are at work even though you're at home can be surprisingly difficult, especially if you don't want to upset them. You simply have to be firm with them. If you are, most will get the point – but some never seem to. All I can say is that if you do find a foolproof method of persuading all these people to stick to calling you in the evening like they always used to, please let me know what it is.

Working from somewhere other than home

Sometimes you simply can't work from home. You can't find the space or you can't find the peace and quiet. Or perhaps your home is badly located – if all your clients are in the local town or city, and you spend most of your time on their premises but need a base nearby to use between client visits, it might make more sense to rent a room in town.

Another reason for finding a base away from home is if your clients are likely to want to visit you. If you live in a smart, clean, relatively quiet home you might be more than happy to invite clients into it. But if it's full of noisy children who leave their toys all over the floor, or you live in a somewhat shabby home, you might impress your clients more with another location.

So if you're not based at home, where should you be? The obvious answer is to rent an office, but you may be able to do better than that. Assuming money is tight, is there anywhere you could use which will be free – or at least very cheap? Do you have a friend with a spare granny flat, or even a spare room in the house they would let you use – perhaps in exchange, for example, for looking after the dog while they're out at work?

You might even know someone with an office they could find you space in. If you work from a client's office, however, and do a lot of work for that client, the Inland Revenue may view you as an employee – unless you pay rent. But this could be a low cost option. Or you could borrow an office only for meeting clients, and work from home the rest of the time. A lot of freelances retain a good relationship with their former employer, and this arrangement can work well.

If you do rent space, it is worth trying to find somewhere which has the use of a photocopier, fax machine, telephone answering service, meeting room and other facilities shared between a group of people and businesses in the same location. Your local enterprise agency can often point you in the right direction (look in *Yellow Pages* under Business Enterprise Agencies).

If you live in a rural district, you may be able to find a local telecottage with space available to rent – a location where a number of people work in their own office but with shared facilities. Some may be freelance, some running their own business, and some even employed but based away from the office. This has a big advantage if you are one of those people who doesn't like to work entirely alone. You have all the social contact you would in an office, chatting over coffee in the kitchen and so on. It's an ideal system for many people.

Working without a base

There is one other option you might want to consider. Perhaps you don't need a fixed office at all. If you're one of those people who is at home with technology, you needn't be at home at all – or anywhere else. With a laptop computer, portable printer and a smart phone, you could even work from your car. You can send and receive e-mails, do your accounts, and print out anything you need to. The phone will take messages if you're not free to answer it, along with a host of other facilities – you can even use it to access the latest test match score. The only fixed base you need is a postal address; some people will still choose to write to you – or put a cheque in the post to you.

A portable electronic office may not be cheap, but it isn't necessarily a lot more expensive than the alternatives, especially if they include renting office space.

Space

It's a fairly safe assumption that you're going to need a desk and a chair. But how much space – or how little – do you need altogether? Of course it depends on your line of work, but the important thing is to see this as two questions:

1 How much space do you need right now?
2 How much space will you need if business takes off?

Money tends to be in short supply when you first set up as a freelance, and you may not be able to afford your dream study from day one. So the best approach is to establish what you can manage on for now, and see how achievable it is. Then compare it with what you would like to have once you can afford it.

The point of this process is to avoid wasting money early on. Suppose you could manage in the spare room for now. What would you need to do there? Well, there's no desk, and you'd have to sort out a bookcase for all your files. And buy a decent chair. And there's no phone point in there at the moment. And you'd need extra sockets for all your computer equipment. It'll cost a bit, but you can manage it.

If you ever have the money, what you really want to do is to finish that loft conversion you never got around to completing, and create a purpose-built study with a big L-shaped desk, lots of built-in shelves, a filing cabinet, and maybe a sofa and coffee table at one end of the room. Of course, you'd have to sort out the lighting and put in a telephone extension, and maybe another line. All rather expensive.

You may not be able to afford your loft conversion yet, but bear it in mind when you adapt the spare bedroom, otherwise you could end up spending far more than you need. You don't want to waste the money you spend now, so try to find a desk which you can re-use in your loft, either as a desk or even as a coffee table with the legs cut down. Get a decent chair which you can carry on using, and if you pay for shelving, make sure you can re-use that as well.

All of this not only saves you money later on, but it also hastens the day when you can move into your loft. You now already have a lot of what you need, so the move upstairs will be less expensive and you will, therefore, be able to afford it sooner.

How little space can you get away with? There's nothing worse than setting up, getting the work coming in, and *then* finding that you just can't cope without more space. So think about what you're likely to need. List everything you will have to find room for. As well as any specialist equipment relating to your work, you are likely to need the following items:

- desk with at least some free space to work on current task
- desk or work surface for at least some of the following: phone/computer/printer/fax
- chair
- shelving for reference books/phone directories etc
- somewhere for admin/finance files
- somewhere for client record files/completed work
- somewhere to keep pens/stapler/hole puncher/calculator etc.
- storage for computer disks
- storage for stationery – spare paper/envelopes etc.
- in-tray (or at least a pile of papers) for work in progress
- waste bin.

You may be able to fit these into a tiny space – you can even keep your books in the living room and your spare paper in the airing cupboard (although I can't tell you how soon this will begin to irritate you) – but you are unlikely to be able to manage with a space that holds less than this. Don't waste time and money trying, and failing, to work in the cupboard under the stairs, when for only a little more money you could have made yourself a comfortable office in the dining room.

CASE STUDY: FINDING A SPACE TO WORK FROM HOME

Elaine Parry had decided to leave her job as a landscape gardener and work for garden design qualifications. Once she had earned these, she wanted to set up as a freelance garden designer. Although she spent a lot of the time out in clients' gardens, she needed a fairly large desk where she could draw up designs and look after the administration side of her work.

Elaine had three teenage children which meant that most of the house was noisy and busy, and impossible to work in.

However, Elaine's eldest child, Heather, was nineteen and at university, and away working abroad most of the holidays. Her bedroom was still there for the times she was at home, but these were very rare at the moment. So Elaine took over Heather's bedroom, replaced the almost empty wardrobe with a large desk with shelves over it, and had a phone line put in. The changes were modest, so there was still plenty of room for Heather when she was home.

What do you need?

Communication

The first category of equipment you are going to need is the wherewithal to communicate with your clients and prospects. There are three key ways of doing this, and you will probably need to use all of them.

Post

You are almost bound to send out invoices if nothing else. If you are a freelance gardener you can probably get away with handwritten invoices, but if you are a PR it will look very unprofessional if they aren't produced on a computer. Only you know whether your line of work demands smart computer-generated paperwork or not. But at the least you are going to need stationery with your name and address at the top of it. You may also need compliments slips and business cards (more about these in Chapter 9).

When it comes to producing outgoing post, you will probably also need a computer with at least a word processing package on it so you can produce smart looking letters.

Phone

You're bound to need a phone, and you'll need an extension at your desk. If you work from home, and especially if you live with other people, it can be very useful to have a second line installed. That way, you can still make calls while your teenage children are on the phone to their friends. If you are sharing a phone line with the rest of the family, you may need to restrict its use. It would seem unreasonable to ban the rest of the family from using the phone at all (even if you could), but you might ask them to use the phone for urgent and/or brief calls only between 9 a.m. and 5.30 p.m.

You can, of course, use a mobile phone for work; but do your costings carefully, since this can work out more expensive. Or you could use a mobile when you're out and about, and a land line when you're at your desk.

If you are going to have letterheads, business cards or anything else printed with your phone number on them, make sure you print the right number. If you decide a fortnight after collecting the stationery from the printer that you're going to put in a second line at home and use that as your work number, you'll have a lot of wasted paper with the wrong phone number on it.

You can choose to have your phone line registered as a business line. This costs more than a residential line, but in exchange you get a faster guaranteed repair time, an entry in *Yellow Pages* and other benefits. If you think this might be worth your while, contact your telephone service provider and check out the details.

Unless you are always at your desk during office hours, you will also need some kind of system for taking messages. If you don't, you could miss a crucial call offering you a major contract. It won't give a good impression when the phone keeps ringing without a reply – the client may put the phone down and call one of your competitors. You might want to invest in an answering machine, or you could use an answering service.

Another service to consider subscribing to if you spend much time on the phone is Call Waiting. This means that if you are expecting an important call you can still use the phone, knowing that if your call comes through you won't miss it (Call Waiting means that a bleep will sound to let you know another call is coming in).

If anyone you live with answers the phone for you when you're out, train them to do it properly, in the following way:

- always be friendly and polite
- take the caller's name, company and phone number, and repeat back the phone number to make sure they've got it right

- note the time of the call
- ask 'Can I tell her what it's about?'
- tell the caller what to expect: 'He'll be back after five o'clock, so you could call him then'; 'She's away until Monday, I can ask her to call you early next week'; 'I'm not sure if he'll be back before the end of the day, but I'll make sure he gets your message', and so on.

Electronic media

If you are freelancing in an office-based job, such as PR, research, writing and so on, it's unlikely that you can manage without a fax machine. This may be integrated into your computer (which you're bound to need), or it may be separate.

If you send and receive many faxes, or only a few but long ones, you may find it makes sense to install a second, dedicated fax line. This is something you can always save until later, once you're sure the expense is worth it, but remember that your stationery will need to be corrected when you do it. If you think it's likely, perhaps you should print fewer letterheads and business cards in the first place, in anticipation of an early reprint with the new number. Although you can't receive non-fax calls on a dedicated fax line, it is useful for making outgoing calls if you want to keep your phone line free for an important incoming call (and you don't subscribe to Call Waiting).

If you want an Internet connection, you will need a modem and a phone line. A second phone line is something you can share between your Net connection and your fax machine – or install a fax modem and receive all your faxes on the screen. If you are connected to the Internet you can also communicate by e-mail. Whether or not you need to make this investment will be determined by whether your clients are connected, and whether they would expect you to be online as well. Once again, if you want your e-mail address printed on your stationery, co-ordinate this with your printing.

Administration

You will need to keep your accounts (which we'll go into in more detail in Chapter 8). You will also need to keep customer records. These may be entries in your address book or lengthy documents, but whatever form they take, you'll have to have them. You will also need to keep bank statements, receipts, bills and so on.

It is a good idea to organise all this information right from the start. Have every file you are going to need sitting ready – empty – before you begin. Files for invoices, files for paid bills, files for contracts, files for bank statements: we'll see exactly what you need later, but the important thing is to have it ready when you first set up. Otherwise you will find, six months down the line, that you have a huge pile of assorted papers and the task of sorting through them and creating files for them all seems insurmountable.

Buying a computer

You will probably need a computer to help you with administration. The subject of how to choose a computer could (and, you will find, does) fill several books. But there are several points worth emphasising if you are buying a computer from scratch.

Ask for advice from people who already have a computer, and who use it for something as similar as possible to what you will be using it for. However (and I'm sorry if this seems contradictory) be very careful who you ask, or at least be wary of their answers:

- Many people will try to tell you that you need whatever they have got – it's human nature. So mark their credibility down a few points if they do this.

- Many people will tell you that you must have all the latest technology, and you absolutely *have* to be on the Internet. Don't take their word for this – ask them why, and think carefully about their answers. (It's probably because they want to come round and play with all the fancy new stuff they don't have themselves.)

- When you ask for advice, observe the other person's response. If they tell you what you want before you have told them what your requirements are, be suspicious of their advice. However, if they start by asking you questions, they are probably a much more reliable adviser.

- Ask advice from as many people as you can until you start to get a clear thread of consistency coming through. Then stop.

Whatever you buy will become obsolete sooner or later (probably sooner). You can't avoid it. So focus on what you need the computer to do for you now, and what you think you may need it to do in the next three to five years. If you can't afford to go on the Internet right now, but you think you may do later, buy one with that capability even if you buy second-hand. But if you're never going to need to produce complicated graphics, don't bother paying extra for software that will give you that ability.

Before you decide to do everything through your computer (and a lot of people will push you to), think about it. Fax modems and e-mail are great for a lot of people, but not for everyone. For a start, you may have to turn on your computer every day just to see if you have any messages. If you use it eight hours a day anyway, that's no problem. But if you only use it one day a week to do your paperwork, it's a bit of a drag. If you have a fax modem and your computer crashes, you have also lost your fax – again, worth the risk for some but not for everyone. A separate fax and no e-mail – at least for the time being – might make more sense.

Allow plenty of time to get acquainted with your new computer. Don't expect that if you assemble it in the morning you'll be working away on it by lunchtime. Give yourself a couple of days to settle in with it.

Don't put any games on your computer unless you have the self-discipline of Mr Spock. Remove all the games that came free with it.

Once you have your new computer, and especially if it's pretty state-of-the-art, you will find that your friends want to play with it. Some of them will even say things like, 'I've got this great new screensaver you're going to love. I'll just load it for you. I only need to reconfigure a couple of things – won't take long.'

Whatever you do, do not let these people near your computer. If necessary, bar them from the house. To them, a computer is a toy – at least, *your* computer is. To you, it is the way you earn your living. You cannot afford this kind of risk. It will only be a matter of time before one of these misguided people does something horrible to your computer and you lose several days' work putting it right. They can be hard to deter, but install a password and reveal it to no one.

Specialist equipment

In addition to all of the equipment listed above, you will also need to invest in any equipment specific to your trade. If you are a media buyer you will need media directories, if you are a designer you will need specialised computer software (maybe even a drawing board), if you are an illustrator you will need paints and brushes, paper and canvas, and so on.

The most expensive equipment tends to be the technology – computer, fax, phone and so on. But you can often borrow or buy second-hand, and costs are coming down all the time. You may well have at least some of the equipment already. If the lists above seem alarming, don't panic. Most people find that with a bit of scrimping and borrowing they can get started for inside a thousand pounds as a freelance (specialist equipment excluded), and upgrade their equipment later when they can afford it. For some people – especially those who don't need a computer – the costs can be far lower.

Summary

- Before starting to invite work, you need to set yourself up with a space to work from and some basic equipment.
- You will need to decide where you should be, i.e. location – whether to work from home or whether to work from somewhere other than home, or even to work without a base.
- Decide how much space you will need to accommodate yourself and equipment.
- Assess what you need in terms of means of communication, such as post, phone and electronic media, and whether to buy a computer and/or any specialist equipment.

4 | USING PROFESSIONAL ADVISERS

When you're freelance, you have to do everything for yourself. You're not only in charge of carrying out the work, you're also chief salesperson, administrator, accountant and personnel manager (you may be the only person, but you're still responsible for your own wages, pension contribution and so on). You have to look after everything from the board room to the post room.

The professionals

It's no surprise that most of us find some of these responsibilities pretty daunting. When this happens, the best solution is to take professional advice – but who from? Obviously it depends on your needs and your own experience, but sooner or later you will find yourself calling on at least some of the following:

- bank manager
- accountant
- solicitor
- financial adviser
- insurance broker
- consultants and other professionals.

We'll look at each of these in turn, and then go on to look at the principles for finding and using professional advisers effectively.

Bank manager

Although it is not a legal requirement as a freelance, you will probably find that it is a good idea to open a separate account for work from your personal account. The Inland Revenue can focus on that account when they come to check your tax returns, and there will be less confusion with any non-taxable income, which will have gone direct into your personal account – such as the £500 your great aunt left you in her will.

Assuming you already have a personal bank account, there are two schools of thought as to whether you should open another account at the same bank or a different bank. There is a strong argument that if you are happy with the service you get from your bank at the moment, you should open another account there.

The opposing argument has two strands. The first is that if both accounts are at the same bank, there is always a risk that sooner or later they will muddle something up, or make a transfer from one account to another to cover an overdraft, without checking with you first. If your new account is at a different bank, this simply isn't possible. The second strand of the argument is far more basic: if your cheque books are issued by different banks, they will be different colours. This makes it much harder for you to write a cheque on the wrong account by mistake.

You'll have to decide which of these arguments impresses you more. Of course, if you are not happy with your existing bank, it is definitely a good idea to open your new account elsewhere.

You can choose, as a freelance, whether or not to register your new account with the bank as a business or personal account. You will be offered a different range of services and bank charges depending on which option you go for. Talk to your bank manager (or sound out more than one if you're still deciding where to open the account) and ask to have the pros and cons of each type of account explained.

Accountant

Since the invention of the self-assessment form for tax, just about every freelance who lacks a degree in accountancy has employed an accountant to fill in the form for them, even if they employ them for nothing else (I know freelances who *do* have a financial background but who still can't figure out the form). The current system demands that as a self-employed person you take responsibility for calculating your own tax (see Chapter 8).

As well as this task, you may also want an accountant to sort out your VAT returns if you are VAT registered, and possibly to keep your books for you. However, as we saw earlier, the chances are that you have relatively few clients and therefore send out relatively few invoices. This means that keeping the books is probably not a huge task, and it might be more economical therefore to do the job yourself.

Solicitor

As a freelance you are probably most likely to use a solicitor to advise you on contracts. If you work in an area where contracts can be complicated, or where you have to look out for legal pitfalls, you may want a solicitor to read through contracts for you. Or you might want a solicitor to draft a standard contract for you to issue to all your clients. For example, suppose you are a marketing consultant and you recommend to one of your clients that they invest heavily in a marketing campaign which, in the event, fails and loses them a lot of money. Wouldn't you feel happier if your client had signed a contract saying that while your advice was given in good faith, you could not be held responsible for the consequences of following it?

Financial adviser

Your financial adviser can help you decide whether to take out life assurance, and what sort of pension you need. The chances are that you would be very well advised to take out some kind of personal pension as a freelance, and pension premiums are tax-deductible.

Your financial adviser and your accountant will need to work alongside each other if they are going to give you the best service possible.

Insurance broker

There are certain types of insurance which can be very worthwhile for freelances:

- Insuring your home – your insurance policy may be affected if you use your home as a workplace.
- Insuring equipment you use for work, such as a computer. You may not be able to claim on your household contents insurance policy for equipment you use for business purposes – this may require a separate policy.
- Insuring against loss of earnings due to accident or illness.
- Professional indemnity insurance. If one of your clients sues you, you could be in big trouble without this. If you are in a line of work where your clients could make a substantial

damages claim against you, this type of insurance is worth taking out.

Consultants and other professionals

You may sometimes need to employ the services of other professionals, but be prepared for the fact that these can work out to be very costly. As a freelance you are unlikely to need them very often, if at all. The sort of consultant or professional you might want to use includes:

- computer consultant
- marketing consultant
- PR consultant
- designer.

When you do use consultants and professionals, make sure you get a clear written quotation from them, and read the small print thoroughly. Make it clear that if the costs look likely to rise you want advance notice so that you can prepare – or take avoiding action – if necessary.

Finding the right adviser

It is important that you are happy with the adviser you choose. You should find someone whom you trust, and someone you can get on with. The most sensible way to go about finding someone is to ask for recommendations. If you know other freelances or people running small businesses, ask them if they use an accountant, insurance broker, or whoever it is you need. Would they recommend them?

It's generally worth asking several people for recommendations if you can. You may get two or more people mentioning the same adviser, or you could end up with a good selection of advisers to choose from. And ask them if they know of anyone they would recommend against.

When you ask for a recommendation, ask your friends or colleagues to comment on the advisers' weak points as well as their strong points. If you have specific requirements, ask if they can comment on those. For example, if you're looking for a computer consultant and have never used a computer in your life, ask whether the consultant being recommended to you is any good at explaining computers in words of one syllable. This way, even if you have several recommendations you should be able to identify the most promising.

What do you do if you can't find a suitable recommendation? Perhaps you need an insurance broker and you simply can't find anyone you know who has used a local broker. If this happens, you could approach your local Business Link (see Business Centres in *Yellow Pages*). These centrally funded organisations offer a central point of contact for a range of business support and advice, and should be able to point you towards a suitable adviser.

The other source of contacts is, of course, *Yellow Pages*. It is unwise to choose an adviser purely at random, but quite reasonable to make an approach without any recommendation and then assess suitability.

Assessing an adviser

The more important the advice or help you want, the more effort you need to put into finding the best person. If you want a computer consultant to give you half a day's training on your new software, it would be a shame but not a crisis if you didn't pick the best person. But if you want an accountant to look after all your finances, it is worth investing quite a lot in finding the best person you can.

There are two angles to take once you have found a potential adviser:

- ■ meet the adviser
- ■ approach existing clients of the adviser for references.

Arrange to meet at the adviser's office; this will tell you a lot. Does it look professional and smart? Do the staff (if there are any) give a good impression? How are you treated? It's hard to say exactly what you're looking for, because you're really looking for a feeling. Does the place make you feel you can trust the adviser, and that you will be well looked after?

Have a list of questions prepared, and don't be shy. If you want to know something, ask – the adviser should have no objections to this. You will want to know what service will be offered and at what price. But you may also want to know other things. Does the adviser have many clients in your line of business – is there a specific understanding of your particular type of problems? Will an insurance broker automatically shop around for the best deal for you every time your policies come up for renewal, or just leave your policies with the initial insurer? Does the computer consultant offer on-site repairs, and within what timescale?

Ask the adviser to write to you following the meeting to confirm the main points of your discussion. Not only does this give you written confirmation of services and charges, but you can also monitor how happily the adviser agrees to write, how quickly the letter arrives, how professionally written and laid out it is, and so on.

When it comes to following up references, ask the adviser for the names of at least two or three. Remember that the references picked will be chosen on the basis that they will paint the best picture, so whatever you hear is likely to be the best angle you could get.

- Call the referees, or write if you prefer, and ask them to give you their view of both the strengths and weaknesses of the adviser in their opinion.

- Ask them how long they have been employing the adviser's services, and how they first met.

- Sometimes you may feel you want to make sure these are real clients and not friends who have been briefed to give a glowing report. Asking how they first met the adviser may help. You can also ask them to be specific about what services the adviser provides for them, and how often they use the adviser. If after this sort of questioning you still have an uncomfortable feeling about the adviser, even if you're not sure anything is amiss, don't take a chance – look elsewhere.

Getting the best from your adviser

Once you have appointed your adviser, you need to make sure that you provide whatever is needed in order for them to work properly for you. If you want top class service, put some time into considering how you can work together to achieve it.

- Identify precisely what you want the adviser to do. For example, suppose you want your accountant to fill in your tax return each year. Do you also want to have your books kept for you? Work out a clear brief in advance, and don't keep changing your mind.

- Ask what information the adviser needs and when, and then supply it. If your insurance broker wants an estimate of your earnings by the end of next week, make sure you sort it out. Your adviser cannot do the job properly if you don't supply the wherewithal, and you are wasting your money if you then don't give the adviser the chance to work effectively.

■ Be honest with your advisers, or they can't do their job properly. Give them the bad news as well as the good. Don't try to hide cash flow problems from your bank manager, for example, or to conceal from your solicitor that a disputed contract was backdated after it was signed.

■ Keep in touch with regular advisers, and keep them informed and updated about any relevant developments.

■ If you have any concerns about your relationship with an adviser, or about the level of service being provided, discuss this openly. If you don't, things will only get worse.

Business advisers are expensive, and should be used with care (and careful budgeting) if your earnings are limited. But as a freelance you are almost bound to find yourself employing their services sooner or later. You may not use many of them, and you may not use them very often, but you can't do everything yourself. Good advisers, used wisely, can be one of your best assets.

Summary

■ When you are a freelance, you have to do everything for yourself, so you need to assess whether you should use the services of professional advisers.

■ You may need to seek advice from a bank manager, an accountant, a solicitor, a financial adviser, an insurance broker, and consultants and other such professionals.

■ It is important that you are happy with any adviser you choose – you should choose someone you trust and with whom you get on.

■ The best way to find an adviser is on recommendation. Failing that, there are many directories and organisations that you can consult.

■ Be sure to assess your chosen adviser and get the best from your adviser.

Part Two
GETTING ORGANISED

5 | MANAGING YOUR TIME

It is much harder to manage your time as a freelance than you might think. There is no routine, and no boss telling you that a report is needed by Friday or that you're expected to visit ten new clients this month. You need to identify what needs doing, establish when it should be done . . . and then do it. Otherwise you'll never get around to writing to new clients or keeping your accounts up to date.

The other big area where you need to manage your time is fitting work and home life together. You need to be able to get on with the work on your desk even when the sun is shining outside. And if you have a family you need to finish work each day in time to see them – freelancing can break up families if you don't organise your time well.

Scheduling the work

You may find that when you first start freelancing, you have plenty of time and you don't feel any great need to organise it. Of course you'll be occupying most of it with trying to recruit clients, but even so, you may well have time to spare. Good – use it to plan the schedule you will adopt as soon as the work starts to roll in.

Creating a routine

It only takes one or two good contracts for you to reach a point where you realise you need to use your time more effectively. So have yourself a routine from the start. A great deal of scientific research has gone into the importance of routine; I shan't repeat it here, but the conclusion seems to be that we function far more happily when we have a routine, and that in the absence of any imposed routine we invariably create our own. (See another title in this series, *Teach Yourself Time Management*.)

The danger, then, is that you will inadvertently create a routine which consists of falling out of bed halfway through the morning, waking up over a cup of coffee for an hour, sitting down at your desk by about lunchtime, and then wondering what to do today.

Far better to make sure that you have the best possible routine by organising it carefully. You will also find that it is far easier to get on with the tasks you dislike if your schedule is telling you to do them now. I'm not saying it makes them fun, or that you can't avoid them if you try – just that it is harder to justify avoiding them and this will help push you towards getting them done.

In order to create a schedule, you need to identify all the tasks which need doing, and make a sensible guess at how long you will need to spend on each one, and how often – a morning a week, two hours a month or whatever. Every freelance job consists of a different range of tasks requiring various amounts of time, but the following items should help you to establish what needs doing and how much time it will take.

Looking for new work

When you first set up, this could well fill most of your schedule. As time goes on, and work comes in, the amount of time it occupies will reduce. But if you have a high turnover of clients, or you need a lot of regular clients in order to make a decent living, you will probably find that this always occupies a lot of your time. Suppose you freelance as a wedding organiser. The odds are that even those clients who have cause to employ your services more than once will at least leave a respectable gap between weddings, which you will need to fill with other clients.

You must not only estimate the time you need to recruit all your new clients, but also the time you invest in those prospects who don't become clients. You can calculate roughly how long it takes to recruit a new client: time spent identifying leads, writing the sales letter, making a follow-up phone call, meeting them (including average journey time), writing a proposal and so on. You know (or you will once you've read Chapter 9) what stages you have to go through. Simply multiply this time by the number of approaches you expect to make.

Experience will help you fine-tune this timing estimate, as you discover what your hit rate is – the number of prospects who convert into actual clients. You may well find that as you get better at judging who are the most likely prospects, so your hit rate will go up. If one in twenty approaches pays off at first, you may begin to notice that the successful ones all have something in common – for example, they are all small companies, or they are all manufacturing organisations. So you start to focus on these and your hit rate goes up.

Even when you have enough work to keep you occupied, you should still maintain some activity in this area. Otherwise, what will you do if your best client goes bust, or gets bought out and has a change of policy about using freelances? If your clients are private individuals, their circumstances could change unexpectedly – they could leave the area, get divorced, go bankrupt or fall under a bus. So always follow up promising new leads and keep them interested, and be on the look out for new prospects to approach.

You will have to decide whether you want to approach new prospects in batches or as a continuous process. You could – for efficiency – send out a batch of letters one week, make follow-up phone calls the next, arrange meetings for the next two weeks and so on. The next month, you start again with a fresh batch of letters. However, if you find that this makes for far too much work in the week you make the phone calls, for instance, you could send out a couple of letters, make half a dozen phone calls and aim to fix up at least two meetings each week on a rolling system.

Real work

Of course, it's all real work, but what I mean by the phrase is the actual work that brings in the money – not the time you spend finding the work, invoicing for it, buying your new computer, opening your post and all the rest of it. If you are a journalist, the real work is the time spent researching and writing articles for which you get paid. If you're an illustrator, it's the time you spend with your pen or brush in hand.

Before you start thinking about going freelance, the assumption is probably that real work occupies virtually all one's time. But the truth is further from this than you might think. As always, it depends very much on the work you do, but as a rough gauge, the average freelance spends only about 60 per cent of the time earning.

Accounts

The amount of time you spend sending out invoices and keeping your books in order will depend very much on what you do. But it is bound to take long enough to deserve a place in your schedule, even if it's only half an hour a week. As a freelance, it's essential to issue invoices swiftly. You need the money – you always do – and you won't get it if you don't ask for it. If you only send out invoices at the end of each month, you can't expect to be paid promptly for the work you did in the first week of the month.

Before you finalise this part of your schedule, check what your main clients' payment systems are. Some of them may, for example, issue cheques at the end of the month for invoices which came in before the 20th of the month before. So don't schedule your invoice session for the last week in the month and then find your biggest client always takes two months to pay.

General administration

This covers everything from opening post to going out to buy the new software you need for your computer, or the new secateurs if you're a freelance gardener, or a new outfit for work if you need to look smart for your clients. You will need to spend time dealing with phone calls querying your invoices, fixing up dates for meetings or sessions with the client, checking train times for your next trip to London or Edinburgh for a PR event and so on. You may also need to allow time for scanning newspapers looking for companies in the news which are worth approaching for work, or visiting trade shows to make new contacts and keep abreast of the latest trends and products in your industry.

A vast amount of the workload in this category is irritating but unavoidable. This is the category into which you should also build an allowance for all the non-work things that happen in work time even if you don't want them to: trips to the dentist, visits from the plumber when your lavatory outflow backs up, and phone calls from friends and relatives who are convinced that now you're at home all the time that means you're always free for a nice chat. I'm not suggesting that you can schedule in all these events precisely, merely that you can guarantee that an average of half an hour to an hour a week will disappear this way, so you might as well make sure that your schedule contains enough leeway for it.

Making your clients feel valued

A good freelance is always a little paranoid. You should assume that your clients are receiving regular phone calls and letters from your competitors touting for work, just as they once did from you. It worked for you – why shouldn't it for them? I'll tell you why not: because you should be spending as much time as it takes making your clients feel that they would rather employ your services than anyone else's.

It may not take long, but it's a crucial investment. Phone your clients to ask if they are happy after you've completed a job for them. If you worked as a researcher giving them information to support a proposal they were putting to the board, call after the presentation and ask how it went. If you're a trainer and ran an important session for a client, check afterwards if they had any feedback or comments. If you're a wedding organiser, call after the honeymoon to see if your clients were happy with the wedding and enjoyed their honeymoon – if you impress them, they're more likely to recommend you to their friends.

It's also a good idea to take your biggest clients out to lunch – or at least for a drink – once or twice a year for an informal chat. Send out Christmas cards, or wedding anniversary cards, or whatever suits your clients. Build enough time into your schedule to do all the things which will make your clients so loyal to you that they won't even bother opening letters from your competitors. It's not luxury time – it is an investment which will be more than paid back by having to spend less time looking for new clients because your client turnover will be so low.

Contingency time

I can't tell you how much of this you need – it depends on what you do for a living. But if your schedule is so tight that you haven't a minute to spare, you'll be in trouble if a client rejects your work and asks you to redo it, or if your computer crashes and you lose two days' work. In reality, this contingency time is largely allocated in evenings and at weekends for many freelances. If this isn't an option for you, because you have family commitments or another job – or you're a workaholic and you're already working sixteen hours a day, seven days a week – be warned. The tighter your schedule, the more of a crisis it will be when this kind of emergency crops up; and believe me, sooner or later, it will.

Arranging the routine

You have now worked out what to do and how long for. But in what order should you do these tasks? It's very much up to you and your own preferred pattern of working, but here are some tips for turning a list of tasks into a schedule.

Make sure that any task which needs an uninterrupted space of time gets it. This might seem self-evident, but if you look at the number of people who don't do it, I guess it can't be that obvious. If you reckon your accounts take three hours a month to sort out, and you can't cope with interruptions, make sure you write into your schedule three hours at a time when you can avoid interruptions. Don't allocate it three hours at a time when phone calls are likely to come in, or on a Monday morning when you have to plan your week ahead, or on a Friday when you may have to deal with things that can't wait until after the weekend.

Most people find it helps to ease themselves into the day with straightforward tasks such as opening post, checking and responding to e-mails, and making phone calls. Schedule yourself time every day to get all these tasks out of the way so you can clear the rest of your time for more solid work. Allocate, say, 9 a.m. to 10 a.m. to tidy up all the little bits of dealing with post and responding to phone messages. Then you can get down to serious work. You're much more likely to get everything done in an hour if you have a schedule which says that you should have finished it by 10 o'clock.

Monday morning – or even all of Monday depending on the work you do – can be a good time to get smaller jobs out of the way. If you are a consultant, you could use Mondays for writing sales proposals and client reports, keeping the rest of the week free for finding new clients and delivering the work. Monday could be your day at the desk, and Tuesday to Friday your days out of the office.

If you are out of the office a lot, try to arrange half an hour at the end of each day back at your desk to deal with anything that has come in – phone messages, faxes and so on – while you've been out. If you can't manage this, at least make sure that you have half an hour each morning to catch up with yesterday's bits and pieces.

Think about the best time for each task. It makes sense to open and deal with your post and check your e-mail first thing in the morning. It makes sense to schedule the real work at a time which suits the client – don't bother scheduling to get up early and be at your client's premises at 8.30 a.m. every day if you work for the kind of people who don't open up until 9 o'clock. If you work for the type of clients who are always in meetings, don't schedule yourself to phone new prospects between 10.30 and 12.30 every morning – you won't get through to them. Make this kind of call before 9.30 a.m., after 5.00 p.m., or perhaps even at lunchtime.

Have a clear work schedule, but don't give yourself such a minutely detailed plan that it becomes unworkable. You don't have to allocate every minute of every day. You're aiming along the lines of something like this:

Daily:

9.00–9.30: deal with post, e-mail, faxes, phone calls and other small tasks

9.30–5.00: main task of the day

5.00–5.30: catching up with today's messages and phone calls

Weekly:

Monday: bits and pieces, proposals etc.

Tuesday to Thursday: real work

Friday morning: pursuing new work

Friday afternoon: admin and accounts

Aim to stick to your schedule as much as possible, but don't worry if it doesn't always work out – be prepared for changes here and there. Suppose your schedule means that you spend mornings at your desk and afternoons out with clients. One of your clients might only be able to meet you at 11 a.m. Fine – just juggle your schedule a bit, or simply miss out on a bit of 'at your desk' time this week. You might have allocated Tuesdays to pursuing new clients, and at 9 a.m. one Tuesday a client calls with an emergency they want you to spend the whole day on. These things happen. At least with a schedule you know which tasks have been overriden, so it's easier to make sure that you slot them back in somewhere else if necessary.

Reviewing your routine

You may find that once you begin to operate your schedule, it has problems you hadn't identified in advance. If you live in an area where the post doesn't arrive until 10 a.m., it's no good scheduling dealing with post from 9.00 to 9.30. You might discover that you want to get invoices in before the end of the month to speed up payment, so some weeks you don't want to leave them until Friday. Maybe your clients seem to prefer phoning you at the end of the day, so you should allow time for this.

When you are starting out, you will probably allow a lot of time – perhaps even the bulk of it – for looking for work. Once the work begins to come in, this time will have to be reduced, in order to give you time to do the work you've drummed up. If things go really well, you might find – depending on your line of work – that looking for new clients occupies very little of your time. Often, you begin to look for more work from existing clients, rather than new prospects. As a freelance trainer, for example, you may find after a while that you rarely need to look for a new client; you want to devote your time to persuading your existing ones to put more work your way. This will involve fewer letters, phone calls and introductory meetings, and more proposals and relaxed ideas sessions with your current clients. This in turn is likely to affect your schedule.

So be ready to review and adapt your schedule if you find it doesn't reflect the best balance of work any more. And be on the lookout for any tendency in yourself to stray from it. If you can't get through the day effectively without a lunch break, schedule one in. If you work better at your desk in the afternoons, your schedule should reflect the fact. There's no point in having a schedule if you can't stick to it – it's important that it should be workable. Otherwise you will begin to ignore it, and you then lose the ability to assess whether you are using your time wisely.

Getting the best from your time

Some people have a reputation among their friends, family and colleagues for being highly organised, while others are considered a bit vague or even completely dizzy. No doubt you know which category you fall into. If you are naturally well organised, you will already be using your time efficiently, although there are always a few extra tips we can all learn which make us that much more effective.

If you are completely absent-minded, however, don't despair. The key to good organisation is getting into good habits, and anyone can learn to do that. You may find it slightly more effort than some, and as soon as you finish work you might find yourself putting the washing in the fridge and the milk in the airing cupboard and forgetting you're supposed to be going out this evening. But while you're at work, you can learn to be as organised as you need to be.

Have an objective for every task

If you don't know what you're trying to achieve, it will take you twice as long to get there. So always have a clear aim in mind. Are you simply opening your post now? Opening it and dealing with it all? Opening it and just dealing with the important bits? To give you another example, if you are writing to a new prospect, what response do you want to the letter? Do you want simply to warm them up for your phone call next week? Do you want *them* to reply to *you*? If so, do you want them to ask for a meeting with you, or do you want them to commission you on the basis of this letter? Your work will be both more effective and more time efficient if you are clear from the start about what you are doing and why.

Prioritise tasks

We've already looked at scheduling your day generally, but within each section of the schedule, what order should you do the tasks in? The best system is to scribble out a list of what needs doing, and then categorise the tasks on it. A lot of people label each one A, B, C or D:

- **A**: tasks which are important and must be done urgently (write the proposal you promised the client would be in the post today)

- **B**: tasks which are not important but which are urgent (pay your car insurance)

- **C**: tasks which are not urgent but are important (book your client's caterer for the PR event you are arranging for next year)

- **D**: tasks which are neither important nor urgent, but must be done eventually (create a template on the computer for producing invoices).

Obviously you need to work your way down the list starting with the As. It might have occurred to you that if you do this, you may never even reach the D category tasks, let alone complete them. And you'd be right. If you notice this happening, clear some time – the last half hour of a Friday, maybe – specifically to get these minor but necessary tasks out of the way.

Set deadlines

Some people work well to deadlines and some cannot work without them (someone once said that for a journalist, a deadline is a lifeline). Even if you're not a journalist, your work may have deadlines built into it. But some jobs don't. Even those which do, have certain tasks without deadlines. So you need to create your own in order to make sure the task gets done.

For example, you might be bad at getting around to writing to new prospects. So set a date by which you will have mailed out a certain number of letters, and another by which you will have followed them all up. It is important to make your deadline realistic. It's pointless giving yourself six months to write ten letters – you obviously won't even start thinking about it for the first five and a half months. But you don't have to decide today that your deadline is 3 o'clock this afternoon. How about doing it by the end of the week?

Once you have set yourself a deadline, write it down in your diary or on a wall planner. Even if you can remember it anyway, seeing it written down makes it that much harder to ignore it.

Keep a detailed diary

One of the best investments you can make when you set up freelancing is a page-a-day diary. Your diary is not just for writing down appointments; you need room to write down everything you might need reminding of which needs doing on a particular day.

If you find yourself on the phone to a client saying 'I'll call you on Thursday morning', the first thing you should do when you come off the phone is turn to Thursday's page in your diary and make a note to call them in the morning. Write yourself reminders in your diary to chase the printer for your letterheads, or send off a proposal, or buy the new issue of a trade magazine you need to read. Deadlines should always go in your diary. And if you find you need it, an advance note of deadlines (e.g. 'One week to delivery deadline for report for XYZ Ltd').

The rule is simple. If a task, however large or small, (a) needs doing on a particular day or at a particular time, and (b) might get forgotten, it should be entered in your diary.

Do the right number of things at once

Time management experts will tell you that you should only do one thing at a time, and of course they are essentially right. It is much faster to do two jobs in succession, giving each your full attention, than to keep flitting from one to another. Don't keep stopping a major task to make phone calls, for example, simply because you keep remembering calls you need to make. Jot down a note of them, and then make them all when you get to the end of the task in hand.

But there is one exception to the 'do only one task at a time' rule. Certain tasks combine beautifully to save you time, and these are worth looking out for and incorporating into your system.

Most of the ones I use involve combining computers and phones. For example, I usually make a quick phone call from my list of calls at the same time that I switch on my computer. This works especially well if I am calling a company where I have to wait for a switchboard operator to answer the phone, and then again for the person I am actually calling to pick up their extension. The delays in this process slot in nicely with keying in passwords or making selections from the screen menu. By the time I've finished my phone call, my computer is booted up and ready to go. This may only save me two minutes, but it saves me two minutes almost every working day.

I have one of those (now antiquated) PCs which I can't use while it's downloading to the printer. So as soon as I hit the print button, I pick up the phone and get another call or two out of the way while my computer is effectively out of commission for a few minutes. With thought, you can often find lots of routine tasks which combine well in this way. Look out for anything with built-in delays to the system, and then find a quick task which slots into these gaps.

Be assertive

Learn to say no to jobs which aren't worth your time (if you're lucky enough to be in this position), invitations from friends to take time off which you can't spare, unnecessary meetings you can't afford the time for when a phone call would do, and any other threatened invasions on your time.

Practise saying no before you do it, if you find it difficult. Think about how you want to phrase it, and then say it out loud a few times until it sounds comfortable. Then pick up the phone and do it for real.

If you're already in conversation with someone and they ask you to do something which you want to say no to but can't quite bring yourself to, have a standard response: 'I'd like to say yes, but I'm not sure whether I can find the time. Let me think about it and I'll get back to you.' Then go away and practise saying no before you do it.

By the way, you will find that a meeting can often be replaced by a phone call, or delayed until you're next in the area anyway, which can save a lot of time. However, don't forget the benefits of meeting clients face-to-face in terms of making them feel valued. Take this factor into account before you decide whether the meeting is really unnecessary.

Set an appropriate standard

Don't waste time doing a job more thoroughly or more perfectly than you need to. Of course you should take care over the work you deliver to clients, but don't spend hours writing all your financial records in fine copperplate lettering, or trying to persuade your computer to insert some fancy bit of graphic at the end of all your letters, which no one but you would miss if it weren't there.

When it comes to delivering work to clients, there's no point exceeding the standard required if it takes much longer. Exceeding the standard a little will impress, but some things just aren't worth it. If you are a researcher and submit reports to clients, make sure they are bound and presented smartly. But don't waste time and money organising a printer to print the title page in gold – your client won't care two hoots. They want the presentation smart and clear, and after that it's the contents which counts.

Learn to deal with paperwork

It's easy to get bogged down in paperwork, so you need a simple system. Here is one. First, deal with every piece of paper the minute it arrives on your desk, otherwise you will waste time looking through the same piles of paper again and again. Do one of three things with each piece of paperwork:

- deal with it
- file it
- chuck it.

Don't put it somewhere and think about it again later. Deal with paperwork as soon as your schedule allows, and be brutal about binning anything you aren't going to need again.

When it comes to filing, you need two locations: your archive files and a pending file. There is only one type of document which should go in your pending file – paperwork which you can't deal with until someone else has taken some action. Perhaps you have a quote from a printer which you can't act on until your client makes a final decision about the design of the printwork you are organising for them. If you're not waiting on anyone else, don't file the thing at all – deal with it.

You should also clear out your files regularly, since they can get clogged up with paperwork you genuinely needed when you filed it, but don't need any longer, such as drafts of reports which you subsequently filed the final version of. The trick to clearing out files is to limit your filing space to the minimum you can get away with. You should manage fine with a two-drawer filing cabinet. Once you can't close it any more, it's time to clear it out – it is *not* time to buy another filing cabinet. You can always keep real archive material on shelves in box files, such as old book manuscripts if you're an author. And of course you can keep a lot of material electronically on back-up disks.

Learn to deal with distractions

These fall into two broad types: distractions of your own making, and other people's interruptions. Distractions you generate yourself include looking out of the window at the sunshine and deciding to sit out in the garden in a deckchair for a bit, remembering a vital football match is being shown live on television this afternoon, and telling yourself that Tuesday morning is really by far the most sensible time to go Christmas shopping.

You will find, if you monitor yourself, that the human mind is amazingly creative when it comes to justifying taking time off for these things. You may be one of those people who is never distracted, in which case skip the next paragraph. But if you're human, sooner or later there will be temptations. You need to find a balance. Can you honestly afford the time – or could you realistically make the time up in the evening or at the weekend? Or have you got work to do which can be done perfectly well from a deckchair in the garden? If the answer is yes, go ahead and succumb. Why not?

But if you can't afford the time, imagine the scenario when you call your client to say you haven't completed the job, or they call you to tell you it's just not up to standard. Frighten yourself into getting on with work. Another technique is to reward yourself: 'If I've got to the end of this by three o'clock, I'll watch the second half of the match.' Or, 'If I'm ahead of schedule by the end of the week, I'll go Christmas shopping *next* Tuesday morning.'

When it comes to interruptions from other people, you need to learn to be assertive – beginning with social interruptions, which are often the worst. Start by telling all your friends and family that you have a 'no phone calls or dropping-in-for-coffee' rule between 9 a.m. and 5.30 p.m. When they break it, be polite but firm. Just say 'I'm terribly busy at the moment. Can

I call you this evening?' or 'I daren't let you in; I'll get behind with work. Why not come to supper on Wednesday?' Remember that if you break the rule once, they will assume that it's all right to ignore it in future. So even if you do have the time this once, think hard before you let them in. A fairly straightforward way to stop visitors dropping in is simply never to answer the door when you're working unless you're expecting a legitimate visit.

When it comes to work interruptions, these should be easier to handle. Generally you will only be interrupted by phone. As soon as the caller tells you who they are, say 'Hello. I'm afraid I'm busy just at the moment. Is it a quick call, or can I ring you back when I've got time to talk properly?' Then fix a time and stick to it.

If you are really pressured with work, just don't answer the phone at all. Let the answerphone or message service deal with calls. You can pick them up when you have time, and deal with any urgent ones at lunchtime or at the end of the day.

Use the quickest method that works

Don't write if you can fax, don't fax if a phone call is quicker. (Faxes can sometimes be faster because you don't get caught in conversation or spend hours holding for someone.) Don't post a letter if you can e-mail. Sometimes you do need to write or fax, but remember that it can take longer and shouldn't be done without a reason. You may find other techniques specific to your work which help to speed things up – be on the lookout for them. Check that they don't:

- add to the overall cost, or
- reduce the standard of work you deliver to your client below an acceptable level.

So long as they meet these two criteria, use them. For example, as a freelance trainer, you may find an off-the-shelf training package which saves you developing one particular course from scratch yourself. You may want to customise it, but it still saves you time. So long as the time saved justifies the cost, and you are still fulfilling the client's brief, go for the faster approach.

Take short breaks

If you spend all day doing the same thing – sitting in front of a screen, weeding someone's garden, correcting proofs, phoning round to arrange events for clients – you are bound to find that every so often you begin grinding to a halt. This is natural. When it happens, take a break. But limit your breaks to ten minutes, which is the most effective time for recharging your mind without totally losing your thread. Several short breaks through the day are far more effective than one or two longer ones.

If you find the prospect of hours of work without a break deeply depressing, build in brief breaks as landmarks. You could always listen to *The Archers* on Radio 4 at 2.00 p.m. while you make a sandwich: it gives you a fixed point to look forward to when your mind can switch off completely from work and recharge for a quarter of an hour.

Sometimes you don't need a break from work, just from the task in hand. You could do a bit of filing, or make a phone call, just to give one part of your brain a rest. I'm not advocating doing several tasks at a time – I'm suggesting an alternative break which is more constructive than making yet another cup of coffee.

Know yourself

More specifically, know your faults. What are your weak points when it comes to managing your time? Delaying settling down at your desk first thing? Taking too many breaks? Too long breaks? Forgetting minor tasks? Chatting too long on the phone?

Be honest with yourself, and then set targets. This week, you will aim to be at your desk five minutes earlier each day than you were the day before. You will go to the kitchen to make coffee a maximum of four times a day. Or you will make sure no phone call lasts beyond ten minutes.

Don't make the targets too difficult or you will give up and achieve nothing. If you have several weaknesses, tackle one or two at a time only. Once you have mastered one, address the next.

Scheduling your home life

If you live alone, and especially if you have no friends, you have it made – as a freelance if nothing else. But assuming you have a life outside work, you will need to fit the two existences together. If you miss out socially, sooner or later you will suffer emotionally, and this is bound to have a detrimental effect on your work. If you have a partner, especially if you live together, it becomes even more important to fit home and work together effectively. And if you have children, too, a life outside work is essential.

Formulating a rule

It's easier than you might think, really. There is only one technique to follow: have a rule and stick to it. Decide when you will work and when you won't, and recognise that if you allow yourself to break the rule, there's no point having it. The critical thing, then, is the rule itself.

First, you need to recognise – and so do your family – the importance of the rule. This is demonstrated by its alternative. Without a rule, or without an effective one, you will allow yourself to take on more work than will fit into a working day. You will do this because you know you have evenings and weekends, and you either enjoy the work or want the money, or are afraid that if you don't take this job, the client will go to someone else and never offer you anything else in the future.

So you work evenings and weekends. You rarely see your partner, and you see even less of your children. You've forgotten you have friends. Few relationships can survive this. Some break up, others pull themselves back from the brink . . . by imposing the rule which they should have had from the start.

So what is this all-important rule? Well, it depends on your lifestyle, but it has two key criteria:

■ it is workable, and allows you enough time to make a living
■ everyone affected by it is in full agreement with it.

You need to agree the hours you will work and the hours you won't. That's all. If you have no children and your partner never gets home before 8 p.m., you might as well work until 8 o'clock yourself. If your partner goes out every Tuesday night, you could agree that you can work Tuesday nights as well. And if your partner works every other weekend, you can. If you want to work until midnight every night and it's all right with your partner, do it. Just make sure that whatever you agree, you are both happy with, and you can both stick to.

If you have children, you are likely to find that you need to set shorter working hours. A popular rule in this situation is no evening or weekend working (e.g. 'the time beyond which all work ends, is after six and at weekends'). You will find that this gives you almost no leeway if emergencies crop up, so you will have to discuss with your family what you do about these. This ranges from making sure that they never happen by building in the leeway during the working day, to suspending all rules during a crisis.

I would offer a word of advice here: if you decide it's acceptable to work late in emergencies, agree what you all think constitutes an emergency. Does taking on too much work count as a crisis? If so, you could do it five days a week, fifty-two weeks a year (assuming you can get the work). What about work which you could turn down, but is incredibly well paid and seems worth giving up the odd evening for? Just remember the criteria: adopt a system which is workable, and which you're all agreed on.

Enforcing the rule

How can you enforce the rule? If you are good on self-discipline, you may not need to. Or if you are scared enough of your partner. But otherwise, I suggest you agree penalties. This should be fairly painless if you do it in advance – you haven't done anything wrong yet, so there's nothing to fall out over. The penalties need to be sufficient to be effective – if you don't mind them you'll simply keep working late and keep incurring the penalties. But so long as they work, pick what you want, flippant or serious. You could agree that if you're not finished by 6 o'clock, you have to do the supper washing-up. Or that all the extra time you spend at work in the evening comes off your starting time next morning – which means you're free to get the children ready for school. Or that if you work over by more than ten minutes you're not allowed to watch the football, or it becomes your turn to mow the lawn, or you have to do the shopping on Saturday, or you have to treat your partner to a meal out.

The only penalty which I would rule out is withholding sexual favours – it's almost guaranteed to split up the relationship faster than working late will, and it's a recipe for disaster. But anything else is fair game.

Review the rule

You and your partner should both be prepared to discuss and, if necessary, adapt the rule if it seems necessary. There's no point having a rule which doesn't work. Perhaps you simply can't make enough money without increasing your hours. You'll have to discuss whether to do this or, even, whether to return to employment either instead of or as well as freelancing. A rule which works well when you and your partner live apart might need adapting when you move in together. As the children get older, it might become more important that you're free earlier in the evening to pick them up from piano lessons or swimming practice.

So make sure you both reserve the right to ask for a review of the rule, and that you are both prepared to adapt if it seems the best option.

Controlling interruptions from the family

We looked at this in Chapter 2, so I'll just recap briefly here. If you freelance from home, and live with other people, there are two main conditions which you need in order to work effectively. One is a location to work in which is well away from everyone, and the other is a system which ensures that it stays that way without constant interruptions.

The ideal location – if you are lucky enough to manage it – is a room set apart from the rest of the house. It might be at the other end of a corridor, or even have another room between it and the rest of the house as a buffer zone. As an example, you might be able to convert the garage into a study and then knock a door through to it from the dining room. During working hours, the dining room can then be out of bounds.

When it comes to avoiding interruptions, once again you must have a rule and stick to it. As we saw in Chapter 2, the family must understand that you are only able to work from home if you are left alone. If not, you will have to use money out of your income to rent an office elsewhere. This will cut into the family finances, and you will be out for longer hours once you take travelling time into account.

If you have a 'no interruptions' rule, you mustn't break it yourself. It's not fair on your children if most times they come into the room you say 'Hello, darling, nice to see you', and one time in ten you bark 'Get out! I'm working'. Be consistent, and let them see that the rule never changes.

Working from home is great fun and very relaxing, and even with a strict system gives you far more time with the family than you would have otherwise. So it's worth setting groundrules which make certain that it works well.

Summary

■ It is much harder to manage your time as a freelance than you might think, so you need to identify what needs doing, establish when it should be done, and then get on and do it.

■ In order to schedule your work, you will need to create a routine. Decide how you are going to divide up your time to carry out such tasks as looking for new work, doing the real work, doing your accounts and general administration. It is also very important to build in 'contingency time'.

■ Once you have arranged your routine, you should stick to it as much as possible, though be flexible and review the efficiency of your routine from time to time.

■ To get the best from your time you should have an objective for every task, prioritise tasks, set deadlines, keep a detailed diary, do the right number of things at once, be assertive, set an appropriate standard, learn to deal with paperwork, learn to deal with distractions, use the quickest method that works, take short breaks and know yourself.

■ In addition to scheduling your work, you will need to schedule your home life.

6 | SETTING YOUR PRICE – AND GETTING IT

What are you going to charge for your services? You may have a rough idea of what other people in the same field charge, but you still need to decide what your price will be.

You also need to consider the terms of payment you need. Do you need to be paid monthly, or in advance, or once-off at the end of the job, or in instalments? Do you need to charge expenses on top, or will that be part of the overall price?

And once you have decided what you will charge, you need to make sure you get it. The vast majority of freelances work for a negotiable fee. You might have a fixed daily rate, but your clients are likely to ask for a discount if they put a lot of work your way, or to ask you to include expenses rather than add them on top. And you're probably nervous that if you refuse you will lose the job. So this chapter is about deciding what to charge and making sure you get the best deal.

Setting your price

The first thing to establish is how much you need to earn in order to make a living. This is your bottom line. Of course you would like to earn more, but if you find you cannot earn even this much, you'll have to rethink the whole idea of going freelance in your proposed line of work. The figure you are looking for is your break-even point.

This should be relatively straightforward (if time consuming) to work out. Simply add up all your expenses, from the mortgage to school fees, electricity bills to car repairs, holidays to food. In fact, you may be able to take a short cut to this figure by comparing what you earn at the moment with what you actually need.

Now you need to establish what daily rate would add up, over a year, to this figure. But before you do this, you need to know how many days a year you will be earning. Roughly speaking, there are about 250 working days a year. But you need to allow some time for days you don't earn: days (or part-days) you spend doing your accounts, chasing work you don't get, chasing work you *do* eventually get, being ill, being on holiday, attending trade events, bank holidays when your clients' offices are closed (if you have to be on site to earn money), days it rains if you're a gardener, days you spend catching up with post and phone calls, even days you work and don't get paid because your client goes bust . . . and so on.

As a rule of thumb, you should estimate as a freelance that you will actually earn money only about 60% of your working time – about 150 days a year. If you're an actor doing voiceovers this figure may be an overestimate. If you're a freelance book-keeper it may be an underestimate. But it's a useful average for most freelance work.

You now have a simple equation to perform. Divide your minimum annual income – your break-even figure – by 150, and you have your daily rate. Suppose you reckon the least you can survive on is £18,000 a year. Divide it by 150 and you need to charge a daily rate of £120.

This is the point at which to stop and review. Is this feasible? What would the market expect to pay? If you really have no idea, call up other freelances and ask them. This isn't as daft as it sounds – in most freelance occupations, if they're at the other end of the country you're hardly a competitor. You can find a *Yellow Pages* for anywhere in the country at your nearest main library to look them up. Or phone round a few potential clients and tell them you're not touting for work – at least not at this stage – but you'd like their advice. Could they tell you what they would expect to pay? (You may not be touting, but if they're looking for someone who does what you do, they'll certainly let you know.)

You may also find that your current employer is a useful source of information. Many people go freelance doing the same kind of work that they have been employed doing, and often their ex-employer becomes one of their best clients. If you are planning to freelance working for private individuals rather than businesses, ask around your friends and see what they would reckon to pay for a gardener, a hairdresser who visited them at home, or whatever it is you have in mind.

As we saw in Chapter 1, you also need to make sure there is enough work out there. It will probably take a while to build up to full-time work (and you need to budget for this), but you should talk to other freelances and to potential clients to find out whether they would be likely to employ a freelance in your field. If you find that all the local businesses prefer to use in-house PRs or trainers or whatever you are thinking of doing, you may need a rethink.

The work that people say they might give you, and the work they actually give you when it comes to it, are not the same thing. So be conservative in your estimate of how much work you will get at the beginning.

Assuming the rate people will pay matches (or exceeds) the rate you need to earn, and there's enough work out there, you're in business. If you find that the going rate for freelances in your field is more than your break-even point – whoopee! However, this gives you a range of prices you could charge – anything between your break-even figure and the going rate. So where on the scale do you want to be?

You might think that you want to charge the going rate, especially if you have something to offer that other freelances don't – such as extra skills if you're a computer programmer. Also, there may be a risk in some lines of work that if you charge less than everyone else your prospects will assume you aren't as good.

On the other hand, you might feel that you could pick up extra work if you undercut everyone else's prices. If most of your competitors are businesses, rather than freelances like yourself, you can explain to your prospects that your prices are lower because you don't have the overheads that your competitors do – this justifies your lower prices, and reassures the prospect that your standards are just as high (if they are worried, without putting the thought into their head if it hadn't occurred to them).

One of the mistakes many freelances make is to undervalue themselves. If you offer a highly skilled service which is very useful to your clients, you are worth a decent fee. Look at it from your clients' point of view. If they have the money and you are giving them something they really need, they may be happy to pay very well indeed for it.

And many people like to pay a substantial price because it reassures them that they are getting quality. When you go into a supermarket, do you always buy the cheapest of everything? Or do you sometimes choose olive oil instead of plain vegetable oil, or Brie when you could buy processed cheese, because you know you'll get the quality you want and you're happy to pay a little extra for it?

There is one further point you should bear in mind when you set your price. It is very difficult raising prices as a freelance. It's not impossible, but you find you have to negotiate every price rise with every client – it's not like being a manufacturer and putting a note at the bottom of your catalogue saying 'Due to the rising cost of supplies, our prices will be going up by 5% from next September'. So don't set your price too low thinking that you can easily raise it later if you need to.

Fixing your terms

Now you've decided what your basic rate is, there are lots of details around it which you still need to sort out: payment terms, expenses and the like. Some of these may be essential to your cash flow or your costs. For example, if you work from home as a PR you are likely to make a lot of phone calls; you may need to charge your clients for these.

Payment terms

When it comes to payment terms you will find that a lot of businesses, especially the very big ones, are very slow payers. They can easily take 60 or even to 90 days to pay. They have complicated systems which involve, for example, issuing cheques on the third Friday of the month following the month of invoice, provided the invoice was received before the 6th of the preceding month. The idea of receiving an invoice in the post and writing out a cheque in response is beyond their comprehension. Of course they have sound business reasons for this approach, but it can seem somewhat harsh on a freelance. (Some organisations have a special, fast track payment system for freelances and very small businesses; such organisations should be cultivated as clients and treated like royalty.)

Getting paid

Unless you have a contract with these large organisations which stipulates prompt payment, you haven't much hope of getting it from them. Your options are:

- to budget for a long delay in payment
- to agree a written contract which stipulates prompt payment
- not to work for organisations which cannot pay you within, say, 28 days.

The advantage of dealing with large organisations is that it is easier to chase payment when the person who authorises it – presumably the client you work with – is not part of the accounts system. You don't have to chase them personally for money; you can call them up and say 'I know you asked for this to go through promptly, and I appreciate it. But your accounts department still haven't issued the cheque, and I wondered whether you would be able to find out if there's a problem?' It feels much more comfortable than having to say 'Why haven't you paid me?'

Having said that, you will have to learn, as a freelance, to chase payments. So long as you remain businesslike, and don't get upset or personal about it, there shouldn't be a problem. Your clients will recognise that if you are chasing them for overdue payments, you are simply doing your job properly.

The best technique is to call them *before* the money is overdue. Make sure you know what the system for paying invoices is (you only have to ask). Suppose you know that cheques are always issued on the last Friday in the month. Phone up the Tuesday before and say 'I know you'll be issuing cheques on Friday. I just wanted to make sure that you received my invoice OK, and that it will be going through.' If they suggest there might be a problem, offer to fax or send them a copy invoice, and anything else they need, in time to pay you on Friday.

How do you want to be paid?

You'll need to decide whether you want to be paid in advance, in a lump sum when the job is completed, monthly, weekly or by some other system. In general, certain jobs are normally paid in certain ways, and it's probably wise to stick to this unless you have a reason to do otherwise. If you are a copy editor, you will normally be paid at the end of each job. Authors are usually paid part in advance of writing – when they sign the contract – and part when they deliver the completed manuscript; sometimes they also receive a third payment when the book is published. A freelance book-keeper would probably be paid monthly, a computer programmer on a lengthy job in instalments, a consultant on a retainer, and so on.

The terms on which you ask to be paid will say something about you to the client. For some reason, a weekly invoice doesn't have quite the same implications of upmarket professionalism as a single fee payable on completion. A weekly bill might be the norm in your profession, and it might well be the right choice for you, but be aware of the signals you give out to clients when you state your terms.

If you charge a single fee at the end of the job, how are you going to calculate it? You can tell the client your hourly, daily or half-daily rate, ask them to agree it with you, and let them know at the end of the job how long it took and therefore how much it cost. Some people prefer to do this, and some freelance jobs – such as proof reading – are traditionally paid on this basis.

However, it does have a disadvantage. If you are a fast worker, you will earn less for the job, which hardly seems fair. If you are a slow worker, on the other hand, your client will be penalised for the fact – hardly fair either. For this reason, I often prefer an adaptation of the pro rata single fee. This involves agreeing with the client what your pro rata rate is, and then agreeing how long the job should reasonably take. So you agree, for example, that your rate is £50 an hour, and that this job constitutes a fair six hours' work. You can then agree that the fee will therefore be £300. You and your client can both budget in advance, you both know how and why you arrived at the figure you did, and no one gets penalised if you don't work at an average speed.

What's more, if you're a fast worker you can get the job done to standard in four hours, leaving two hours free to do other work. This is perfectly acceptable, since the client has agreed that £300 is a fair price for the job. For single fee jobs, you are not being paid for your time, but for your skill. You only estimate the number of hours' work as a means of calculating what the finished job is worth.

When should you invoice?

Having completed the job, when should you put the invoice in the post? If you're a gardener, you may have an agreement with your clients that you bill them at the end of each month for the hours worked that month. But if you don't have a standard date for invoicing, when do you do it? The answer is, as soon as possible. The sooner you invoice, the sooner you get paid – so why wait? It seems a bit cheeky to bill the client before they've had time to read/test/use/see the completed job. So the best policy is to complete the work, give the client time to phone you and say 'This isn't what I wanted at all!' and – assuming they haven't done so within 24 to 48 hours – put the invoice in the post to them.

Expenses

Your expenses may include basic materials (such as delegate handouts and training materials if you're a trainer), travelling expenses, phone calls and so on. You have four options when it comes to deciding who pays for these:

■ pay for them yourself
■ bill the client for them at cost
■ charge a higher, inclusive fee to cover the cost of these expenses (but make exceptions for such things as plane trips to Paris or long, peak-rate phone calls to Singapore if you think these are a possibility)
■ use the expenses as a negotiating tool.

We are about to look at the techniques of negotiating. You will find that if you want room for manoeuvre in your bargaining, expenses are often a useful way of creating it. You can say 'I could do it at that price, but I'd have to charge expenses on top'. Or you can put up your prices (in effect) by saying 'I am managing to keep my fee the same, but in future the price won't include expenses'.

If you do the kind of work where you have to negotiate fees, it is often a good idea to avoid mentioning expenses until you are into the negotiation. That way, you keep them in reserve to bring out when you need them as a trade-off or a concession.

Negotiating the fee

If you offer secretarial services, you probably work for a fixed hourly or daily rate. If you are a proof reader, your clients probably tell you what they pay proof readers and you can take it or leave it. But in many freelance lines of work – writing, designing, illustrating, consultancy, research and many others – you will have to negotiate fees with your clients.

Some of us are born negotiators. Most of us, however, find the prospect quite daunting, and it is a frequent source of angst to many freelances. Even once you get into the swing of it, sooner or later someone will ask you to do a job which is quite different from your usual run of work, and you'll be clueless about how to negotiate this one.

There are, however, a few basic rules of negotiating which are straightforward to grasp, and once you know them will ensure that your negotiations are much more confident, happy discussions, which you are very unlikely to come out of finding that you've agreed to work for the next six months for a rate well below the bread line.

Your skill as a negotiator can make a substantial difference to your earnings. For some jobs, you could make literally three or four times the money you otherwise might simply by knowing how to negotiate. So it's well worth learning the skill.

The win/win principle

Understanding the psychology of negotiating is critical. Most people regard a negotiation as a battle, from which will emerge a winner and a loser. It is a point of principle for them to be the victor, quite apart from the other issues of money, time and so on which are involved. It would be shameful to come out having lost the battle.

So your job is to make sure that the other party comes out victorious – at least in the other party's own mind. Allow the client to feel that you have been beaten down and lost the negotiation. You will be able to read the other person's approach if you observe his or her behaviour. The more competitive, the more of a victory the other person needs to achieve in order to sign off the agreement.

Of course, you don't actually emerge defeated at all. It's all a game really – but it's an important one, because it can make a big difference to your income. The idea is that you both emerge feeling like winners. The simplest trick for this is to ask for more money than you ever intend to agree, and then let the other side beat you down until they reach the fee you actually wanted to get. Suppose you want to be paid £600 for a job. You ask £1,000, they negotiate you back down to £600 and you're both happy. This has the significant advantage that they may in fact only talk you down to £750. That leaves you much better off than if you'd simply asked for £600 and stuck to your figure, and they still think they've scored a victory. That's win/win.

You don't have to create a feeling of victory in your client over the main fee. The point at issue may in fact be the delivery date, or the details of the work: as a gardener, you might say that for £5 an hour you will weed, but you won't mow lawns or do major pruning for less than £7 an hour. Your client talks you into doing the pruning for £5 an hour, while you still hold out for a higher hourly rate for mowing, which was what you were really after all along.

Know your bottom line

There is a point below which it is not worth doing the job. If you were offered £1 an hour for computer consultancy, it wouldn't be worth it. If you were offered £1,000 an hour, it probably would be. These are extremes, and only you know the point in between where it switches over. It is important that you know this point precisely before you start negotiating.

The thought of turning down work because it doesn't pay well enough can be terrifying, but you have to be prepared to do it. You might work for very little at the start, just for the experience. But however low – or high – your bottom line is, you must know it and be prepared to stick to it.

It might involve a number of factors, of course. You might decide that you won't do this research job for less than £500, unless the client wants a verbal report only and not a written one. In that case, you would do it for £375, but no less. But you are still being clear about your minimum terms.

A clear bottom line actually makes negotiating far easier, because – so long as you know you will stick to it – you don't have to worry that you'll leave the negotiating table with a deal that is actually going to cost you money. There is a tendency to think that if you turn the client down this time, the client will never offer you work again. But if you are not going to be paid enough to make it worthwhile, why does it matter if the client never offers you any more work?

Saying 'no' to a client seems very scary. I can only tell you that the first time you ever do it, you will find (assuming you set your bottom line wisely) that you actually feel rather good afterwards. You might also feel nervous about losing the work, but you will nevertheless feel a flush of self-respect and confidence.

If your client was never going to pay anywhere near what you needed you have lost nothing anyway. If the client was prepared to offer something close to your bottom line, you will often find that by saying no, and meaning it, you push the client that last little bit of the way to meeting your minimum level after all.

One word of warning, however: never call the other person's bluff by saying no before you have been negotiated down to your bottom line. If you say no in order to push them up a little further, they may not bite. Then you either lose a job you wanted, or you have to backtrack. Once you start to backtrack, they will realise they have you on the run, and they will beat you right down. And they will mark you down as a bluffer, which means they will always suspect you in future of crying wolf.

Find all the variables you can

Before you go into the negotiations, find everything you can possibly use to bargain with:

- the delivery time
- the delivery format
- support from the client (such as the use of a researcher, office space, and so on)
- any perks (such as use of the subsidised cafeteria while you're working on site)
- the number of meetings (which some clients love to organise, and which can eat up your time; stipulate that the fee includes only, say, two meetings and any others will be charged separately)
- expenses
- terms of payment
- . . . and divide the job up into as many chunks as you reasonably can, so you have plenty to negotiate with: 'If I only did a written résumé of the research findings, and the full report was verbal, that would keep the cost down . . .'.

Look at all the variables before you agree to anything

Make sure that the client gives you a full brief before you give a price for the job. Suppose you agree to doing the research for £250 and *then* you are told that the client wants two bound copies of the report. It's very difficult to put your price up at this point. So make sure you have asked all the questions you could possibly need to before you commit yourself.

And when you do give a price, always recap: 'So you want me to research the views of hoteliers about your proposed new product. I'll talk to twelve hoteliers in the South West, and ask them each the same ten questions which we've already prepared. I'll put their answers into a written report, and I'll submit two bound copies of it to you. The fee will be £300 including the presentation copies, plus the cost of my phone calls.'

Aim high

If you don't ask, you don't get. Ask for as much as you dare – you may be amazed what people will pay. If they don't argue, they would almost certainly have paid more. So ask for more. No, of course you can't say 'It'll cost you £1,000' (no objection from client). 'Sorry, what am I saying? I meant £2,000'. But you can say 'It'll cost you £1,000 . . .' (no objection) '. . . plus expenses'.

There is an old story about a canny optician training his assistant and explaining: 'When a customer asks what their new glasses will cost, you say "They come to £50". If the customer doesn't wince, you add ". . . per lens". If they still don't blanch, you say "And the frames will be £75".'

The trick with negotiating is to be prepared. Have all your extras thought through in advance. For example, '£250 for the basic research . . . plus expenses . . . and another £50 if you want two bound presentation copies of the report . . .' and so on.

You have to be prepared for the opposite response, of course. If you aim high, the client may balk at the price. In this case, you can bring out a list of compensating factors: '£250 for the basic research' (at which the client balks) '. . . which of course includes all basic expenses . . . and two presentation copies of the report, printed and bound. If you don't need the presentation copies, you could save £50 . . .'. Never drop your price without a reason, but prepare reasons for doing it if you need to.

Make trade-offs, not concessions

Don't agree to anything without making sure you get something back in return. If the client asks for something, make sure you get something back before you commit yourself: 'I can deliver in two weeks so long as you are happy to wait another week for the extra copies . . .' Or, 'I won't need to charge for the expenses if you can let me use an office here for three days to make the phone calls from . . .'

Summary

■ As a freelance you need to decide what you are going to charge for your services. You will need to do some research to find out what others in your field charge.

■ In addition to setting your price, you need to fix your terms and make sure that your clients pay you on time.

■ Negotiating your fee is a skill that you need to learn – operate on the win/win principle.

7 | TOO MUCH WORK AND NOT ENOUGH TIME

This is a chapter which we'd all like to need. You might think, when you're starting out, 'I should be so lucky!' But in fact, too much work can be a serious problem for a freelance, despite being obviously preferable to the opposite state. If you decide to turn work down, you think to yourself every time 'I'll probably never work for them again'. And sometimes you're right, I'm afraid.

But if you do have more work than you can handle, you'll have to find some way of either offloading or turning down work. There are various options when you find yourself in this position, some of which involve turning work down, and some of which don't. Some of these options can work in combination: you could, for example, turn down some work *and* offload other tasks.

There are two basic solutions to the 'too much work, too little time' problem. Either you have to reduce the amount of work, or you have to expand the amount of time – which you have to do by using other people's time as well as your own. So these are the two types of approach we'll look at.

Reducing your workload

There are only so many hours in a day and sooner or later, if you are successful, you will inevitably find you have filled them all up. If you have made a deal with your partner that you will not work outside certain hours, you are going to have to make a complementary deal with yourself that when your time is full, you will make yourself deal with the problem. It can be hard when you first run up against the problem – it is very tempting to take on the work anyway and kid yourself you have time for it. So you must be ready to face up to the problem, or all your promises to spend time with your family or friends will be broken.

There are techniques for cutting down the amount of work you are offered, which we'll look at in a minute. But the simplest way to reduce your workload, of course, is simply to turn down some of the work you are offered. But which work? And how do you say no?

Which job should you turn down?

When it comes to deciding what to turn down, you may not have much choice. If you are committed to maximum capacity, and someone offers you more work, that is obviously the only job you are in a position to reject. But often you do have more choice than this. You may not yet be committed to some of the other work – you may know that a certain job will be coming in shortly, but it hasn't yet been confirmed. In these situations, you often can choose whether to say no to the latest job you are offered, or whether to take it and turn down the job you know you will come up shortly.

The exercise is never as simple as it might sound. You find yourself having to decide whether to turn down one job before you are sure the next job is going to happen. For example, if you are a voiceover artist, a film company might ask you to do a (well paid) day's work next week. Another, regular client has told you that a week's work is coming up, but they don't know yet if it's going to be next week or the week after. The pro rata rate is lower, but as it's more work the final fee is higher. Do you take the one day job or not? Don't ask me: no one can make this decision for you – it goes with the job of being a freelance.

There are more factors to consider than simply which job is most likely to come off. Should you turn down a smaller job from a promising new client in favour of a job from a client who is regular but doesn't pay very well? In Chapter 9 we'll look in more detail at the number and balance of clients you should aim for; you should certainly take this into account when deciding which work to take.

The safest option is to imagine the worst possible scenario, which is that the client you turn down may never give you any work again. This doesn't often happen, but it does sometimes. So you are balancing not only this job but all future work from one client against another.

Sometimes you can phone the client whose job is not confirmed and explain the problem: you'd rather take their work, but you don't want to turn down the other work and then find you have neither job. They will be pleased that you would rather work for them and are trying to keep your time free for them, and sometimes they will be happy to give you a decision about the work sooner than planned. But they may simply not be able to confirm the work in time for you, and you'll still be left having to make the decision on the basis of hopes and hunches.

Saying no

When you do have to say no to a client, how do you do it? The best approach is to let them see that you are being very professional, and that you would rather not work for someone at all than risk delivering work that isn't up to standard. Explain that you are committed elsewhere, and it wouldn't be fair on the other work which you already have to jeopardise its quality by taking on too much. The implication should be that if, in the future, you have committed yourself to this client, they can be sure that you wouldn't jeopardise *their* work either.

You want the client to be left with a feeling that here is a real professional, who won't compromise the work they take on, who insists on delivering work to a high standard, and who is so much in demand that they are turning work down.

The fact is that very few regular clients will stop using you if you turn them down once. The more work they give you, the more they will want to stick with you despite finding occasionally that you aren't available. In any case, finding someone else they are happy working with can seem like a hassle to them. If you turn the same client down again, they are more likely to look elsewhere – and the more often you tell them 'no', the greater the chances you will lose their business permanently. It's the first-time clients you say no to who are least likely to come back to you.

The only note I would add about regular clients is that they sometimes feel slighted. If they consider themselves one of your best clients, they might feel you ought to give them priority. You probably do when you can; the thing is to make sure they realise it. A phone call when you see the problem on the horizon is useful for making the client feel valued as well as for helping you make a decision. If you phone and explain you'd rather work for them but you need an assurance that the job will go ahead, they can hardly complain if you turn them down later because they didn't give you that assurance.

Juggling

Freelances are usually excellent jugglers. In a sense, this doesn't belong under the heading of 'turning work down', but it is at the moment when you are about to turn work down that you find you really need to do your best juggling.

It is quite often possible to shift schedules around so that you can fit everything in. This is rarely an option if your work requires you to be in a particular place at a particular time – as a wedding organiser you can hardly ask a client to move the date of the wedding for you when the honeymoon has already been booked. However, most freelance work is much more flexible than this. As a trainer you can often ask a client if it might be possible to reschedule a training session, given enough notice.

Sometimes you can fit in work by extending the deadline on it. If a client says 'Can you do this research for me by the end of next week?' you might have to say no. On the other hand, you could say 'I can't do it for then, but I could do it for the end of the month.' Sometimes this won't be good enough for the client, but sometimes it will.

Or maybe you could do some of the work, if not all. Either you can do less work, or you can finish it off later. As a photographer, for example, you could offer to do studio work only, even though you don't have time to do the location shots. Or you can do the photo session when the client wants, and produce the contact prints, but you can't actually run off the enlargements for another week or two.

Changing what you do

One of the ways of reducing your workload is to shift the focus of the work you do. Suppose you work as a freelance business writer, writing press releases, annual reports, customer newsletters, brochures and so on. After a while you find that newsletters are by far the best paid part of the work. Once you've secured the work, it keeps coming in regularly – every quarter or every month or however often the newsletter comes out – without you having to go and chase it again. And each one is a substantial job with a substantial fee; not like a press release which only takes an hour to write and the fee reflects the fact. What's more, the newsletters can be great fun to work on.

The time comes when you simply have more work than you can handle. One of your options at this point is to decide that from now on you will focus on newsletters. You will stop being a press release and brochure writer, and you will become a specialist newsletter writer and editor. You will still have to say no to work to achieve this, but it gives you a criterion for turning work down, and ensures that by doing so, you end up with work which you find more fun and more lucrative, rather than simply easier to schedule.

Depending on your workload, you can make this shift in more than one way. You could:

- give all your clients plenty of notice that you will no longer be available for this kind of work as you are specialising from now on
- retain your existing clients for all types of work, but don't take on any new clients except for newsletter work
- retain your best clients but give notice to the rest of them that you will no longer be writing brochures and press releases
- continue to do smaller jobs but only for clients for whom you also write newsletters.

Many jobs give you the option of specialising after a while, and being a specialist often gives you the opportunity to put your prices up – you're now an expert, after all, and can price your skills accordingly. I would suggest that you choose to specialise in an aspect of your work which is either very lucrative or really interesting, and ideally both.

Putting up your prices

The other classic way to reduce your workload is to increase your prices. This will mean that you either lose some clients, or that your existing clients give you less work. The object of the exercise is to reduce your workload, so you have to raise your prices to a level which will have this effect. The end result should be that you are still working full time (but no more), and that you now have more money to show for it.

The trick is to put your prices up the right amount to achieve this. There is a fear that you will put them up too high and *all* your work will disappear. However, there is an easy way around this. Freelances don't publish price lists, so there is no need to charge everyone the same rate. Your clients probably have no idea what you are charging everyone else. In any case, you may well negotiate a different fee with each of them already.

You can put your prices up for new clients only. Or for only those existing clients who you feel will be prepared (if reluctantly) to go along with it. Or for the clients you don't enjoy working for and feel need to pay well to make it worth your while. Or for everyone all at once – it's up to you. Test the water with one or two clients if you like, and then go ahead and break it to the rest of them.

Assuming you haven't put your prices up recently, your clients aren't going to be that surprised. They know you have a living to make; their salary has probably gone up more recently than your prices, so deep down they know you're being reasonable. The best way to break it to your existing clients that your prices are going up is well in advance. Warn them in November, for example, that your prices will rise at the end of the financial year, in April. They have plenty of notice, and it's difficult for them to kick up a fuss over something that isn't going to happen until next year. By the time April comes round, it's difficult for them to start arguing when they've known about the price rise since before Christmas.

If you are still nervous about putting your prices up, find ways to make it look like less of a jolt to your clients (while still making enough difference for you to reduce your workload but not your income). For example, tell them that your basic fee will remain the same, but you will now be charging expenses on top, instead of including them in the price. Or charge the same but for less work, and make them pay extra for the additional work. For example, as a computer trainer offer a standard service of four one-hour sessions instead of six for your basic fee; the client can still have more sessions but you will charge these separately.

Offloading work

If you don't want to turn work down when the load gets too heavy, that's fine. In this case, you will need to find someone else to share the load with you. There are various ways in which you can do this, each of which have their own plusses and minuses.

The biggest difficulty with offloading work in general is that, as a freelance, your clients tend to feel that they are paying for *your* skills and *your* time, not someone else's whom they may not have the same confidence in. The extent to which this applies varies according to the work you do, but it is virtually one of the things which defines a freelance, as we saw in Chapter 1. If you are an illustrator, and a publisher commissions you to illustrate a book, the publisher doesn't want to find that the illustrations are done by someone else entirely because you passed the work on. At the other end of the scale, if you are a freelance book-keeper, most of your clients are unlikely to mind if you pay someone else to do some of the work for you, so long as it's accurate.

You will have to judge what you can and can't ask someone else to do, and whether or not you should tell the client. If you offer secretarial services, and you pass on some typing to someone whose skills are equal to yours, your client probably doesn't mind and doesn't need to be told. But if you are a PR your clients will choose you on the basis of your personality and your understanding of the kind of PR work they need. They may well have chosen you *because* you are freelance; if they had decided to use a PR company they wouldn't have known who in the company was doing the work, and they couldn't be sure that it would always be someone they were happy with. In this case, they would probably be quite put out if they found you were offloading work onto someone else without telling them.

It is a very bad idea to conceal this sort of thing from a client deliberately in case they are unhappy about it. If they find out that you are hiding it from them, they'll be even more unhappy. So either offload work they won't mind you offloading, or ask them first, or find some other way to reduce your workload.

Passing on specific tasks

One of the simplest ways to overcome the workload problem is to pay someone else to do parts of the job for you. I'm not talking about employing someone, since that would effectively mean you were starting a business – which is one of your options, but one we'll look at in a moment. I mean effectively paying another freelance. For example, as a gardener you could pay someone else to do lawnmowing for you, while you do the more skilled work such as weeding, pruning, planting or landscaping.

You will have to negotiate what you will pay them; you could end up paying them less than you get paid, in which case someone else has done the work and you've still come out on top. You may simply pay them the same rate as you; you don't get the money, but then you don't have to find the time to do the work. This may well be worthwhile – they might do 10 per cent of a job enabling you to get paid for the other 90 per cent, when the alternative would have been turning the job down because you just didn't have time to do that last 10 per cent. When this is the case, it can even be worth paying out more than you are getting paid – if you have to – in order to be able to say yes to a job of which you will do the bulk yourself.

The chief difficulty with this method of offloading work is that it can be very hard to find any part of your work which you can successfully offload. Suppose you're a writer. It's not easy to find other people who are also skilled writers, and have a sufficiently similar style to your own that your clients will be happy with the finished work. In theory you could offload some other aspect of your work – but what? You write straight onto the computer, so you wouldn't use a typist. You could get someone to type your invoices for you, but that only takes ten minutes a week.

As a copy editor you can't offload parts of a manuscript, because part of the job is checking the continuity of the whole thing, the consistency, and any cross-references. And only another skilled copy editor would be capable of doing a good job of it anyway. So unless you subcontract whole jobs (which is an option we'll look at later), it's hard to see what tasks you could usefully pass on.

However, for some work this is a useful option. A trainer could pay someone else to type, copy and collate training materials and handouts. A researcher could find someone else to spend a day at the library looking up addresses, or doing other basic aspects of the research. A wedding organiser could use a freelance of some kind to spend a day on the phone making calls and sending out standard letters to confirm arrangements with suppliers such as caterers.

It's worth mentioning that partners and teenage children can be very good at stuffing envelopes, making phone calls and so on. They may lack the skills or the motivation that you want, but if you only occasionally need to offload work, and their skills match your requirements, keep this in mind. Teenagers may hate work, but they love money, and sometimes your own family are genuinely among the best skilled people around and they may know your work better than most.

For example, if you are a photographer and have a daughter who is learning the skills from you, she may reach the point where she can do your developing work for you when you're very busy, leaving you free to go and take the photographs. A partner who can type will often be more use to you than a freelance typist – they know your work, understand the jargon, can read your writing and so on.

Passing on work

By passing on work, I mean saying to your client 'I'm afraid I'm not available to do this job in the time you want it, but I know someone who can.' Of course, this depends on you knowing another freelance or company in the same line as you. Some freelances use this technique quite often; chauffeurs, for example, who are booked for specific times. If you're already booked for Wednesday evening, you can't juggle the work around, so you have to say no. Rather than leave the client to find someone else on their own, you make a recommendation. This means that you come across as being more helpful, and the arrangement is reciprocal so the other chauffeur will be doing the same thing for you. If you do this with regular clients, they will probably come back to you again. If they are new, they may stick with the other chauffeur in future; however, you will have acquired potential clients from your colleague in the same way, so on balance nobody loses out.

If you pass work on, you do have to be prepared for the fact that you may lose the client permanently to the person you pass them on to. However, if the alternative was turning the work down, what have you lost? This is also a very useful technique for turning down work by changing what you do, which we looked at earlier. Remember the freelance writer shifting focus to writing newsletters only and giving up writing brochures and press releases? Instead of just saying to a client 'I don't do that kind of work any more', it's far more helpful to say 'I don't do that kind of work any more, but I know someone who does'.

Subcontracting work

We looked at passing on specific tasks a moment ago – typing, basic research and so on. But when you pay someone else to do an entire job for you, you are subcontracting the work to them. You are employing their services, as you would a carpet fitter or a surveyor, so they are not an employee. You agree a fee, they do the work, you pay up.

Since you are not doing any of the job in question yourself, you want to pay the person you subcontract less than you are paid by the client, or you will lose out. After all, you still have to find the work and negotiate with the client, and take responsibility if the work isn't delivered on time or isn't up to standard. So you have earned a cut. Unless you are particularly keen to hang on to a client and daren't turn the job down, it is rarely worth subcontracting if you are paying so much that you don't get a cut.

The chief minus point about subcontracting is that you do not give up any responsibility for the work. If you use someone who is unreliable or less skilled than you thought, you will have to take the blame, or sit up all night redoing the work. Then you will have to argue with the person who did the work badly, or late, about whether you are prepared to pay them. So choose carefully when you subcontract.

Beware the danger of cash flow problems, too. You are likely to be invoiced for the work at the same time you pass it back to the client and invoice them. If the client is a bad payer, what do you do? Can you afford to pay your subcontractor promptly before you've received the money from the client? And if not, how long will you make them wait? If they wait too long, they may decide not to do any more work for you in future, which could be a considerable loss, as it is often very hard to find good, reliable people you can put work out to.

Do you tell the client you are subcontracting? The guidelines for this are really the same as for deciding whether to tell the client you are passing on work. If the client is likely to mind: check with them first. If they couldn't possibly tell the difference or object, you needn't tell them. If you do decide to let them know, emphasise the fact that responsibility remains with you, and that if there were any problems – which you're sure there won't be – you would put them right within the client's time restraints.

Starting a business

There is another option if your workload becomes consistently too heavy, and that is to give up freelancing altogether. Take on employees, either full time or part time, trained in your skill or another complementary skill such as secretarial work, and start a business. I'm not going to go into the details here of how you go about setting up a business (you can find out all you need to know from another book in this series, *Teach Yourself Setting Up A Business*). The question is: is it the right move for you?

The advantage of starting up a business is, of course, that you can take on more work. If the cost of employing people is outweighed by the increased income, it must be financially worthwhile. If being busy, successful and having a high income is what motivates you, this may well be the best course.

For some people, however, there are other considerations. There are two main aspects of running a business which many freelances see as disadvantages. First, there is the hassle. Once you employ people you have to conduct interviews, worry about PAYE, schedule staff holidays, and a host of other things. Some people choose to freelance because, among other things, they want a simple life. If you are one of these people, you might find that the increase in income is not worth the effort and hassle involved.

And second, many freelances thoroughly enjoy the work they do. If you simply take on a secretary, you have more time to do the bits you enjoy. But if you set up a business, as you expand you will need to take on other people who do what you do – and you will find that you are spending increasing time running the business while other people do the work you used to do.

As a designer, for example, you could end up with a business which employs three or four designers and a receptionist/secretary. You might spend your whole time on administration, recruiting new clients, doing the payroll and the VAT, filling in forms, buying in new equipment, chasing late payments, scheduling your team's time, working out quotations and so on.

Many people find they love doing this, but some people realise after a while that deep down they enjoy designing more than anything else, and they haven't had a chance to look at a drawing board or a computer screen in months. If this is you, starting a business may not be the right option.

If you have too much work, and a good balance of clients, you are in a position of success. If you want to stay a freelance, you can always find some way to turn down or offload work, and still fill your time doing work you enjoy and earning a decent living in the process.

Summary

- If you fortunate enough to have too much work and not enough time, you will need to find ways of reducing your workload.
- You can reduce your workload by turning down work, juggling your projects, changing the focus of what you do and by putting up your prices.
- You can also offload work by passing on specific tasks, passing on complete projects, subcontracting work, or deciding to set up as a business.

8 | **MONEY MATTERS**

As a freelance, book-keeping is far simpler than it is if you run your own business. But you still need to keep basic accounts, and to know how and when to issue an invoice. This chapter is about what you need to record and how. You may also need to register for VAT, so this chapter also explains what this entails.

As a freelance, the Inland Revenue will regard you as being self-employed for tax purposes. You will have to complete a self-assessment form (or pay an accountant to do it), and you will also have to pay your own National Insurance contribution. This chapter will provide a brief run-down of how the tax system works if you are freelance.

It will also look at other financial commitments you might choose to make such as a personal pension, house insurance and insurance in case you have to take time off work.

Keeping accounts

Accounts are only records of what has gone on in the past – they don't tell you anything except what has already happened. They won't tell you how much money you are going to make in the future, or how much tax you could save if you treated your accounts differently, or where the best place would be to invest your money. They are simply records of what you earned and what you spent. Let's look at what accounts you need to keep and what accounts you might want to keep.

Accounts you need to keep

For every transaction you make in your business you must keep a written record to prove it to either the Inland Revenue or the VAT inspector. It's no good saying you spent £137.20 on car repairs if you don't have a receipt to back up your claim. It's no good saying you only earned £3,000 if you don't have invoices to demonstrate this. So every time you buy something for your business get a receipt. If you get a receipt you can claim. If you don't, you can't. So engrave it on your mind: *get a receipt every time.*

Conversely, whenever you receive payment for services rendered you must *give* a receipt, and keep your own copy. This may simply entail writing 'paid' on an invoice that you previously sent out, or you might actually write out a receipt for money you receive. If you don't give receipts you cannot prove how much you have earned. If you can't prove your income the Inland Revenue may believe you have something to hide – such as earning a lot more than you declare – and quite rightly so. This could mean you will be penalised and a higher assessment of your earnings made. And that means you pay more tax.

Accounts you may want to keep

Obviously you want to know how you are doing financially. So you will want to keep some clear record of money in and money out, rather than just a pile of invoices and receipts to add up at the end of the year. You'll presumably want to keep track of who owes you money and whether they have paid. And you may want to keep a petty cash system for small purchases you make from time to time, although there really is no need to do so unless you want to. You will also want to know what you are spending – and the various areas that the expenditure can be broken down into.

For instance, you may well want to know exactly how much you spend on stationery. You may like to know at the end of a year that you spent £23.60 on brown envelopes and £13.42 on white envelopes. You could be even more knowledgeable and know that you spent £12.26 on big brown envelopes and £11.34 on small brown envelopes.

How much or how little information you want to keep is entirely up to you and the dictates of your work. But it is worth bearing in mind that less is more. The simpler the accounts you keep – and the less time you spend doing them – the more time you have to do other things, such as earning the money in the first place.

The Inland Revenue

There are two ways of viewing the Inland Revenue: as ogres to be fought against, deceived and swindled, or as a necessary fact of life. They are not ogres. Don't treat them as such. When you first start freelancing go and see them. Ask what records they would like you to keep, in what form and how often. They are there to be pestered. Phone them up every time you aren't sure of something. Ask in advance before you make costly mistakes. Try to establish a personal relationship with your own inspector. That makes it a lot easier to ask for someone by name, and to be able to use their expertise to get your financial records simple, accurate and legal.

Every year you will have to provide the Inland Revenue with information. Basically they will want to know what you earned, what you spent, and how much profit you made. (Let's assume that you won't make a loss.) You will be taxed on your profit. It's a good idea to put money aside as you receive it ready for paying your tax bill. It is probably wise to put aside 25 per cent of everything that comes your way. If your eventual tax bill comes to less than this, the remainder is a bonus – you can view it as a sort of savings scheme. It is unlikely you will have to find more than your 25 per cent until your earnings start to get very comfortable.

If you put money aside every time you earn any you won't have to scrabble around finding tax money when it is due. Nor will you have to phone up the Inland Revenue and explain that you are going to make a late payment, which will incur penalties, fines and interest. Put the money aside and sleep nights.

VAT

Again, like the Inland Revenue, VAT inspectors are a fact of life. If you earn above a certain amount a year – currently around the £50,000 mark – you have to register for VAT. This means that you have to add a little something (currently around 17.5%) to every invoice you send out. This money then has to be paid over to Customs and Excise. The good thing is that you can deduct from this money any VAT that you have paid on any equipment or goods you have bought. If you aren't registered for VAT you obviously don't make a payment and can't claim anything back.

If you think you should be registered, phone straight away and ask for advice. The VAT inspectors are, contrary to their reputation, usually very helpful and co-operative. Like the Inland Revenue, they only turn nasty when they think someone is being deceitful, using creative accounting, trying to make them look silly, or just being plain dishonest. Keep your records straight and even a VAT inspection will not worry you – in fact you will feel a great sense of pride when they give you the thumbs up.

National Insurance

When you are self-employed, which is how freelances are categorised for tax purposes, you have to pay your own National Insurance (NI). If you contact your local office (listed in *Yellow Pages*) they will tell you exactly how much you should pay each month. It's probably best if you set this up on a standing order. This is your basic cover, and is called Class 2 NI. If your income exceeds your outgoings you are also liable to pay Class 4 NI. This is calculated as a percentage of your profits (in other words your income) and is collected by the Inland Revenue at the same time as your tax – it appears on your tax bill. National Insurance contributions are not tax deductible expenses.

Your accountant

Do you need one? A while ago the answer may well have been no. Now, however, there is the terrifyingly complex tax 'self-assessment' form to fill in each year, which is so complicated that most people find they need an accountant to help them understand it.

Having an accountant can be a valuable time-saver. When you first set up they can advise you on what records you need to keep. As you are going to have to pay them quite a lot at the end of the financial year to complete your self-assessment form, it makes sense to ensure that they have your records in the form which they want and understand. The less time it takes them to do your accounts the less money you have to give them.

What records?

As a freelance, the records you have to keep should be pretty simple. Assuming it's just you, and you work for relatively few clients, the records you need are straightforward. You will need a system which records:

- money in
- goods bought
- running costs
- possibly a petty cash system.

You don't need to record your wages – you simply don't get any. How will I be paid? I hear you wail. Your wages are taken from your profits. So you can pay yourself something each week or each month out of those profits. These payments are called drawings. You may cash a cheque for the same amount each week or month and spend it, or draw money from your bank or building society as and when you need it.

You don't need to keep a record of this money but it might be helpful to do so – then you'll see where all the money goes. What you must not do under any circumstances is spend *cash* which you are given as payment for work done. Bank the cash after giving a receipt and recording it, and then draw money for your personal use.

Money in. Do you get paid in cash? Or issue invoices? Or both? Whatever you do you will need a cash book. This can be as simple as you want and it's still called a cash book even if you only receive cheques. You can probably buy a ready made cash book from a local stationery shop; remember to get a receipt as it is a tax deductible expense (we'll look at these in more detail later). It has to record:

- the date on the invoice
- the amount you receive
- your invoice number or cash receipt number
- the date you received the money
- any cash paid to you and when you banked it
- some sort of reference so you know who paid you
- any VAT element if you are registered
- the amount less the VAT, if you are registered

Figure 8.1 is an example of an entry in a cash book.

Invoice date	Amount	Invoice/ receipt no.	Date received	Date banked	Reference	VAT	Amount net of VAT
18/03/98	£3,000	ME23	16/04/98	16/04/98	Mr Howe	£525	£2,471
31/03/98	£28.75	R35	14/04/98	16/04/98	Casual	£5.03	£23.72

Figure 8.1 Specimen entries in a cash book

This simple book tells you at a glance who owes you what and what you are getting in. It doesn't tell you what sort of work you did for people, but it contains enough information to satisfy your accountant if you have one, the Inland Revenue, and the VAT inspector.

Money out. In order to work effectively you are going to have to spend money. You may need to travel, invest in equipment, pay rent, heat and light an office or study, and pay for postage and stationery. These details need to be recorded in a purchase book. Again this can be as simple or as detailed as you want. A simple way to organise this is as follows:

- the date you receive an invoice or request for payment
- a reference such as the name of the supplier
- when you paid it
- a reference of your own
- the amount
- the VAT (if you are registered)
- the amount net of VAT.

Figure 8.2 is an example of entries in a purchase book.

Date	Supplier's reference	Date paid	Own reference	Amount	VAT	Amount net of VAT
23/05/98	British Telecom BT123-07-K	30/05/98	Phone 14	£125.90	£22.03	£103.87
27/05/98	Morris Envelopes M895	28/05/98	Stationery 56	£48.76	£8.53	£40.23
31/05/98	Plum Computer Ltd PC45/3	31/05/98	Office equip 6	£2,000	£350	£1,650

Figure 8.2 Specimen entries in a purchase book

If you buy a purchase book you will probably find the left-hand page is roughly the same as above. The right-hand page will give you blank columns that you can fill in so that you know what each area of expenditure comes to at the end of the year, as in Figure 8.3. You can then see at a glance what each area is costing you to run and at the end of the year you can total up these columns and give the information to your accountant.

Equipment	Heat/ light	Travel	Stationery/ post	Telephone	Computer	Rent
				Phone 14 30/05/98 £103.87		
			Stationery 28/05/98 £40.23			
					O/equip 6 31/05/98 £1,650	

Figure 8.3 Specimen entries in a purchase book of total annual expenditure

The money you pay out and keep a record of should be tax deductible. This means that at the end of the year you are allowed to add up all your work expenses, and subtract this sum from your income to give you a figure which is your net income. You are only taxed on this net figure. So if you earned £20,000 you don't have to pay tax on all of it. If your tax deductible expenses come to £4,000 your net income is £16,000 – and this is the figure you pay tax on.

Tax deductible expenses are those which are incurred in the pursuit of your work. You can't claim for a bar of chocolate even if you get hungry during working hours, eat it during working hours, or only have to have a sugar hit because of the stress caused by your work. The Inland Revenue will say that you would have got hungry, needed to eat and incurred some stress even if you weren't working.

A claimable expense is one that you only incurred because you were occupied in the freelance job you are doing – expenses such as buying equipment, heating and lighting an office, buying a computer, or buying stationery which is wholly used in your work. A good accountant can advise you on exactly what you can claim for as a tax deductible expense; it will depend partly on your line of business. A freelance gardener could claim for a new wheelbarrow, but a freelance computer programmer couldn't.

When you first start out as a freelance you will need to buy basic equipment and tools: maybe a computer, a desk, a telephone and equipment related to your specific work. You may well have to go out and buy these items; get receipts for them as they are tax deductible. But what if you already have these things? You can still claim the value of them as start-up costs – effectively what you do is sell them to yourself and give yourself a receipt. Make sure you only charge the real value, though. If you claim your old computer is worth £2,000 when it is no longer worth more than £200, you could get yourself into a lot of trouble.

You can claim for most of your legitimate business expenses each year. But there are some – known as fixed assets – for which you have to spread the cost over several years. A fixed asset is one which you don't simply get the benefit of once, like a box of envelopes, but one which continues to benefit you for several years, unless you decide to sell it. Fixed assets are things like your computer, a vehicle you use for work, or a filing cabinet.

Your accountant will treat these expenses differently from the others, because they will spread the cost over several years. For instance, if you've bought a new computer for £2,000 they will not take that figure as a total. Instead they use a calculation called depreciation. Instead of claiming the entire amount in one year, you claim 25% in the first year and 25% of the balance in the second year and so on for each subsequent year.

What is an invoice?

An invoice is a request for money to be paid. Other people's invoices will just arrive on your doorstep with your post and all you need to do with them is record them – and pay them.

But you have to send out invoices if you want to be paid for your work. You will need to have them printed or use your computer to print them out. You need to include some important information on them if they are to work effectively. You need:

- your name and address (including e-mail if you use it)
- your phone and fax numbers
- the date you are sending it out
- a reference number
- the name and address of the person to whom it is being sent
- the work done

■ the amount (both in total and with the VAT separated out if
you are registered)

■ the terms of payment

■ any discount for prompt settlement.

You also need to head your invoice: INVOICE/STATEMENT. A statement is a
regular (often monthly) bill which totals up all the invoices since the
previous statement, for payment all at once. For this reason, some
businesses have a policy that they only pay on statements and not invoices
(on the grounds that they're still waiting for the final statement). So make
sure they don't have this excuse for not paying you by making it clear that
what you are sending is both an invoice *and* a statement. A typical invoice
might look like the example in Figure 8.4.

Fred Mullions
Steeplejack
The Old Chapel
High Street
Worcester WO3 9LP
Tel: 01234 567890
Fax: 01234 567899
E-mail: fred@server.net.co.uk

INVOICE / STATEMENT

Date: 07/05/98

Ref: FR12

To: Father Mitchell
       St. Anne's Church
       High Street
       Worcester

For:	Repair to church steeple	1,200
	VAT	210
	TOTAL	**£1,410**

Payment terms: 28 days
There is a 5% discount if payment is received within 14 days

Figure 8.4 Specimen invoice/statement

You might have to add more information if the client needs it, such as an order number. This is a number or reference given to you when the person asks for the work to be done and it is their authority to commission the work. They might be a large organisation and their accounts department wouldn't pay an invoice without such an order number on your invoice. You might also want or need to include more details of the work done with a breakdown of different areas such as:

For work to steeple	900
Erecting scaffolding	100
Clearing away old tiles and making good	200
Total	**£1200**

It all depends on what the person requesting the work needs. The advice, as in all things to do with accounts, is keep it as simple as possible – more is less.

Your accounting procedure

The simplest accounts procedures usually work the best. An ideal system would be:

- Have a cash book in which you record every invoice you send out in numerical order with details of to whom it was sent, what the work was, and the amount.

- Mark this book with a tick when the invoice is paid.

- Have a series of envelopes marked 'post', 'phone', car', 'rent', 'electric' etc. Put into these envelopes each receipt or confirmation of payment as you collect it.

- Once a month, or once a week if you feel you need to, add up the contents of these envelopes and write the totals in a purchase book, with the date.

- Once a year add up all the invoices.

- Once a year add up the 12 monthly entries you will have made for each envelope.

- Keep a record of anything else such as pension payments, loans, interest payments.

- Hand over the cash book, purchase book and other records to your accountant at the end of the year.

Sit back and relax knowing you are free to get on with your work, your accounts are done, you have a moderately simple accounting system that is basically foolproof, and you are on top of it all.

What the Inland Revenue wants to see

When you get your tax bill, usually six months after you've submitted your accounts, it will be in two parts – usually two equal instalments. These are due on 1 January and 1 July of the year following the date of the tax bill. If you are late you will be penalised with either fines or accrued interest – or both.

The Inland Revenue also demands that you keep records for a minimum of six years – this means you must keep every receipt and account book safely, somewhere, for a long time; you are legally obliged to do this. The sort of things the Inland Revenue will expect you to keep are:

- all your account books
- bank statements
- building society statements and pass books
- cheque stubs
- copies of all invoices
- loan agreements
- all personal bank statements and mortgage details
- all receipts
- VAT returns if you are registered
- any other financial information including joint accounts with any partners, shares, interest payments, land holdings and trust funds.

Computers or not?

Some advice given to me many years ago about accounts and computers was that if you have a system and it is working, you don't need a computer. And if your system isn't working, a computer will make it worse a lot quicker.

So do you need a computer to do your accounts? Probably not, unless you are very computer literate, have a large turnover, generate an awful lot of invoices, keep a lot of customer records and have effectively moved from the realms of freelancing to running a small business.

There are, however, many excellent software packages on the market which might enable you to do your accounts moderately easily and quickly. Remember though that any system is only as good as the operator. And if you are spending time learning the ropes on your computer, that is valuable time you could have spent generating new business or completing projects.

Any software you decide to use must be easily assessable by both the Inland Revenue and the VAT inspector. It must also be understood by your accountant. It's no good supplying a disk to your accountant and saying it's all on Apple Lightning Express Accounts Mk 2 when your accountant's computer only speaks IBM FigureFun 97. It's almost always best to keep it simple and have a few real books to write in, so your accounts can't get lost somewhere in the vastness of cyberspace.

Insurance and other things

Sorry, but you need it. If you try to manage without, sooner or later you'll find yourself regretting it. The basic cover you should consider is:

- accident insurance
- equipment insurance
- life insurance and pension
- permanent health cover
- professional indemnity insurance
- vehicle insurance.

In more detail:

- *Accident insurance*: This is insurance to cover you in the unfortunate case of losing a finger, hand, leg or eye. What sort of cover you need is up to you but for a small monthly premium you get cover in any eventuality and the amount paid out should replace any lost income resulting from the accident.

- *Equipment insurance*: Any equipment you use in your freelance work should be covered against fire and theft. The premium is usually a yearly one and can sometimes be linked into your home contents.

- *Life insurance and pension*: If you die you certainly lose an element of earning capacity. Whilst you might not think you have a need for money once you've gone, your family certainly will – and probably more than before. The easiest way of taking out life insurance is to link it into your pension plan. So if you die early your dependants will be taken care of – and if you don't you can retire happy in the knowledge that you have an income. Life insurance is not normally tax deductible but pension plans are – which is another good reason for linking them together. An ideal aim is to spend around 8 per cent of your profits on your pension plan.

■ *Permanent health cover*: So you don't cut a finger off but you do get appendicitis and have to take a couple of weeks off work – who pays your wages? No one, that's who. That's why you need permanent health insurance. If you get sick you still get an income coming in. Cover is usually a monthly premium, around £50, and you'd get around £1200 a month if you became ill and couldn't work.

■ *Professional indemnity insurance*: If you are, for example, a consultant and one of your clients claims that your bad advice has cost them a lot of money, they may decide to sue. And you may not be able to pay up if they win their claim. Professional indemnity insurance covers your costs in this kind of case. Don't do without it if your line of work means you could face a claim from a client. It is usually paid as an annual premium.

■ *Vehicle insurance*: You should have your car covered as a private person, but what about the business use? If your insurer finds out you had an accident while using your car for work, you probably won't be covered. It is better to make it legal and get business cover for the times you use your vehicle to deliver products or whatever.

Insurance brokers exist to get you the best deal, advise you, deal with the claims, fill in the paperwork and let you sleep nights. Find a good one by personal recommendation or through your accountant or bank, as we saw in Chapter 4.

CASE STUDY: THE DANGERS OF NOT KEEPING ON TOP OF YOUR ACCOUNTS

Ellis Callan was a freelance consultant. He kept very basic accounts – just the minimum his accountant had advised him that he needed to keep. Ellis didn't enjoy book-keeping, so he did it as rarely as possible, letting the invoices and payslips pile up for a while, and only sitting down to enter them all in the book once every couple of months. Then he had a rather unpleasant shock. He was about to go on holiday, and needed to take a fairly large sum from his business account – and there was barely any money in it.

It took Ellis three hours to go through his backlog of paperwork and sort out what was going on – three hours he could ill afford when he was trying to get ahead in order to take holiday time off. It turned out that a large invoice from a key client had never been paid, and was now five weeks overdue. Ellis called them: they had never received the invoice.

After that, Ellis set aside a few minutes every Monday morning to keep his books. He found it took very little time so long as he kept on top of it, and he always noticed if any payments were about to become overdue, and chased them by phone. Now he always knows how much money is in his business account, and he doesn't have unpleasant surprises any more.

Summary

- As a freelance, you need to keep basic accounts and know how and when to issue an invoice.

- The Inland Revenue regards a freelance as self-employed for tax purposes. You will have to complete a self-assessment form and also pay your own National Insurance contribution. You may also need to register for VAT.

- Your records should be simple and straightforward. Your system should record money in, goods bought, running costs and possibly a petty cash system.

- Appropriate insurance cover is essential. The basic cover you should consider is: accident insurance; equipment insurance; life insurance and pension; permanent health cover; professional indemnity insurance and vehicle insurance.

Part Three
GETTING THE WORK

9 | **FINDING AND KEEPING YOUR CLIENTS**

You aren't a freelance if you don't have any work. So how do you get it? Well, you have to start by knowing how much work you're looking for, and from whom – the size and balance of clients you want. Then you need to identify the right prospects to target. And having done that, you must get out there and sell your skills. Finally – but essentially – you have to use every trick in the book (or in this chapter) to make sure you hang on to the clients you've got.

How many clients?

If you have too many clients, you won't have time to do all the work. If you have too few, you won't earn enough money. So it's important to have the right number of clients, or as near as you can manage. But what is the right number?

The answer isn't as simple as it might be because not every client gives you the same amount of work. Some are regular clients whom you spend a lot of time working for, while others only give you two or three jobs a year, and small jobs at that.

Categorising your clients

The best approach is usually to categorise your clients into three groups. Let's call them grades one, two and three:

- ■ *Grade one*: These are your big clients, who you make most of your money from. They are your bread and butter. If you lose even one of these it worries you; losing two at once brings on a feeling of panic. If you're a journalist, these are the papers for whom you write a regular, weekly column, and perhaps regular features as well. You are on a contract and can rely on the work coming in as long as the contract is renewed. As a dressmaker, these clients might be bridal shops which regularly put work your way.

■ *Grade two*: These are the clients who give you regular work, but it is less frequent and less lucrative than your grade one clients. You don't worry too much if work dries up from one of these clients, but if two or three dried up at once you'd feel you should do something quite urgently to replace the work. As a journalist, these might be magazines which ask you to write a fairly well paid feature once a month or so. A dressmaker's grade two clients could be mostly private clients who can afford, and like, to have their outfits individually made to their design. They might also include one or two bridal shops who do most of their dressmaking in-house, but put some of it out when they are very busy.

■ *Grade three*: These clients only give you work very occasionally; if one of them stopped giving you work it might take you a while to notice. For example, a trade magazine might ask you to cover the occasional trade fair and write a short feature for a fairly modest fee, or a consumer magazine might use you to cover occasional stories in your region when their regular journalist for your area is unavailable. If you are a dressmaker, these clients might be private individuals who don't order whole outfits, but quite often want alterations or repairs done, or a simple scarf or skirt run up.

The precise balance of clients is up to you to judge, but the important thing is not to put all your eggs in one basket. If you have only two grade one clients, and one goes bust, or changes policy and takes on an in-house designer, for example, instead of using you on a freelance basis, you've lost a huge chunk of work – and income – which it could take a long time to replace.

Broadly speaking, for most freelance work, you should be looking for a balance of clients somewhere in the following range (you'll have to decide whereabouts within the range):

■ Grade one: four to six clients
■ Grade two: six to twelve clients
■ Grade three: ten to twenty clients.

Replacing clients

You will always find that you have the occasional week when half of your biggest clients all want urgent work done at once, and you just have to cope. But if these times become frequent, you should recognise that you have too many big clients. You may have to use one of the solutions in Chapter 7 for dealing with too much work. In the long term, you need to make a note that if you lose any of your grade one clients, you don't want to replace them.

If, on the other hand, you lose one or more clients and *do* need to replace them, one of the best options is often to 'promote' another client. Try to elicit more work from your most promising grade two client, so that they move up to grade one. You may not always manage this, but it is usually far more straightforward than trying to recruit someone completely new.

Often you will have been considering this for a while. Perhaps, if you are a copy editor, one of your clients has been asking for more time for a while and you've had to decline. Now you can go to them and let them know you could take on more work. Or, as a trainer, you've wanted to suggest to a client that they introduce a proper induction training for all new staff, but you've been reluctant to suggest it before now because you knew you didn't have the time to plan and implement it.

Selecting your prospects

Before you start trying to recruit clients, you'll have to decide which businesses or individuals to approach. You can waste a lot of time trying to sell your services to people who couldn't possibly want them.

Your former employer

The first place many prospective freelances go to look for work is their current employer. You explain that you are considering becoming freelance, and ask them if they would consider using you. Often this suits them very well, and you will want to point this out to them. It may be that they don't really need you full time, and they could pay you a higher pro rata rate than they do now, and still spend less on you than they do now.

For example, perhaps you work in the marketing department, and are particularly skilled at spotting problems and opportunities and finding ways to overcome the problems and exploit the opportunities. This is a very valuable skill, but not a full-time requirement in most marketing departments. It's worth paying you full time in order to have access to your skills, but a fair proportion of your time is spent on other tasks.

In this situation, your employer might well leap at the chance of letting you go to become a freelance marketing consultant, and then using your services on a freelance basis. They get everything they want from you at a much lower cost (even though you might increase your pro rata rate considerably – working for twice the price, say, but for only a quarter of your time). You, meanwhile, get paid more to do the parts of the work you enjoy, and you don't have to do the rest at all. And you have plenty of time to earn more money doing the same for other companies.

Many people go freelance in order to get out of the corporate rat-race, without necessarily having a clear idea of exactly what they want to do. If you are in this position, you really want to think about two things:

- What is your organisation currently paying outsiders to do that you could do better or cheaper (or both) as a freelance yourself?
- What does your organisation do in-house that it would make more sense to put out to a capable freelance who understood how the organisation worked?

New prospects

Before you approach people, you need to do some serious thinking about what kind of people to approach. Do they need to be wealthy? Or are you offering an essential service which they have to get somewhere – publishers have no choice but to employ proof readers; a wedding couple are almost bound to use a photographer.

Do they need to be a particular type? If you're a designer, will you find that big companies always have their own designer or design department, and you need to approach medium-sized businesses?

The better you do your thinking, the clearer will be the picture you have of the most likely prospects. I'll give you a few examples:

- As a gardener, you will need to approach people who have some disposable income, whose gardens are quite large (or they could manage them without help), and who have an interest in gardens (or they would just grass it all over and be quite happy).

- As a computer consultant, you will probably want to approach businesses which are growing fast and therefore adapting or upgrading their equipment to keep pace.

- If you're an author, you need to find publishers who take on new authors and who publish books of the type you want to write – children's fiction, business textbooks or whatever.

- If you are a wedding organiser you need to find couples who are planning their wedding well in advance, who want a big enough wedding to need an organiser, and who have enough money to pay someone to organise it for them.

- As a PR you need to find businesses which are big enough and public enough to need some PR work, but which don't have their own PR person in-house. You might find that businesses which employ a marketing manager who either has no department, or has only a secretarial assistant, are just the right size to be interested in using an outside PR.

Once you start to bring the work in, you are likely to discover a pattern in the people who employ you. You will notice that they fall into one or two distinct groups, and in future you can focus on these types when looking for new clients. For example, as a book-keeper, you might discover that most of your clients are in the manufacturing sector. As a portrait painter, you might notice that you are almost always commissioned by parents to paint their children. As a computer tutor, you may discover that your private clients are generally over the age of 50.

Selling

So where do you find these prospects, now you have a profile of what you're looking for? Well, you can make contact in one of two ways. Either new prospects come to you, or you go to them. If you don't know how to find them – all sorts of people need photographers, for example, and they don't wear signs on their foreheads – you need to encourage them to come to you. But if you can identify your prospects yourself, don't wait for them to come to you – get out there and approach them yourself. Or you could use both methods: approach the prospects you can find, and get the rest of them to come to you.

Getting them to come to you

In order to do this, you need to let prospects know you are there. So this approach is all about advertising. You can advertise in the local paper, in the parish magazine, in specialist magazines, in business directories, or by using brochures or leaflets distributed through letterboxes or through other relevant outlets – as a freelance gardener you could ask to put a pile of leaflets in the local garden centre; as a computer tutor you could distribute leaflets through local computer sales outlets.

The trick here – again, one that mostly involves thinking hard – is to advertise in the right place. And the right place is wherever your prospects are going to be looking. The more closely targeted your advertising is at the people you want to read it, the more effective it will be. If you are a freelance typist and you advertise in the local paper, over 99 per cent of the readers will have no use for your services. The few who do may not read the ad. You would be much better off advertising in the local Small Business Club magazine – a much higher proportion of the readers are likely to want your services.

What's more, if you were looking for a freelance typist, would you look in the local paper? Probably not. You'd be much more likely to look in the Small Business Club magazine, or in the *Yellow Pages*. So those are the places where you should be advertising.

The key rule for advertising is to imagine that you are one of your potential clients: where you would look – or where would you notice an ad, even if you weren't searching for it? People who want weddings organised look in wedding magazines; people who want actors look in *Spotlight*; people who want business trainers look in personnel and training magazines or in local business directories; people who want an Alexander Technique teacher look in the *Yellow Pages*, and so on.

Putting your ad together

Assuming you decide to advertise in order to attract clients, there are effective ads and ineffective ones – and you need to make sure yours fall into the first category. An ad doesn't necessarily need to be large or expensive to work. Again, think from your prospects' point of view. What will they notice? And what quality will they expect? If you are a software engineer and you decide to advertise in business computing magazines, it's probable that any likely prospects reading the magazine – business people who want to find a good software engineer – will be looking out for ads. So yours doesn't need to be huge to catch their eye.

The other consideration is what your competitors do. If lots of computer software engineers are advertising in the magazine, and the others all take a full colour quarter page ad, your two inch black and white ad might make you look like a bit of an amateur. When you look for potential suppliers in the *Yellow Pages*, do you sometimes decide to phone the ones with the bigger ads on the grounds that they are likely to be more professional or reliable? I know I do, and I suspect I'm not alone.

However, if everyone else in your line of work takes small, inexpensive ads, you can do the same without losing any impact. If there is scope to compete you don't have to pay more for a bigger, brighter ad – you just make sure the content of your ad is well written.

There is a simple formula for writing good ads, which has acquired the acronym AIDA, which stands for:

- Attention
- Interest
- Desire
- Action

Attention. The first thing your ad must do is attract reader attention. The way to do this is generally to use a headline which tells them not what you do, but what you can do *for them*. Stress the benefit for them of using your services. So don't head your ad 'Secretarial Services'; head it, for example, 'Need to offload some of that typing?' If you're a wedding organiser, stress that you can take the hassle out of the wedding ('Get someone else to do the worrying for you'). If you're a gardener, appeal to the reader's dislike of weeding, or the problem of finding time to mow the lawns. As always, look at the thing from the prospect's viewpoint.

Interest. Once you've caught the eyes of readers, hang on to it. Reinforce what you've just said (but don't waste time repeating it). You could say, for example, 'I can do your copy or audio typing, take dictation, organise your photocopying and even return your reports to you proof read and professionally bound.' Consolidate and expand the point you make in the headline. Let them see that the headline is only a taster.

Desire. The idea is that by the time your readers have got to the end of the ad, they already feel they are a client. You've given them a feeling of how much better, easier, quieter or less fraught their life would be if they employed your services, so they don't want to give it all up by not getting in touch with you. Write in the second person ('You'll have more time to get on with the jobs you really want to . . .'), and keep stressing the benefits for the reader.

Make sure you emphasise the things which are likely to matter to your readers. Don't keep telling them how cheap you are if most of your clients are millionaires. Don't tell them you're quick if time doesn't matter to them. Think about why they would use your services. If you offer secretarial support, they probably want to free up time spent typing for tasks they consider more important. If you garden, most of your clients will need help because they just can't find the time to do everything themselves. If you're a book-keeper, they may be concerned that they don't have the skill to do the job accurately for themselves. These are the desires you should be appealing to: the desire to use their time more effectively, reduce their workload, be confident that the work is being done professionally.

Action. Your readers are now fully engaged, and they can't think how they've managed up to now without secretarial support, a gardener, or someone to keep their books. They're itching to get in touch with you. So the final part of the formula is simple – tell them what to do. Give them a phone or fax number or an address. How will they want to make contact? If they are likely to want to call you on the phone, make sure you print a phone number as well as an address. If your clients are likely to be computerised – perhaps you are a computer consultant – give an e-mail address. Just don't fall at the last hurdle by making it difficult or impossible for your prospects to come to you.

Design. When it comes to the amount of text you want in your ad, make sure you give yourself plenty of space. If you can't afford a big ad, that's fine: just don't write a lot of text to go inside it. The two important factors are the size of the headline, which should be as big as you can comfortably make it, and the amount of white space you leave around the text. It is the space which draws attention visually to what is inside it. Your prospects are far less likely to notice an ad in which the headline has been squashed up and the text printed in small type and squeezed up to get more in. Less is more.

These guidelines for producing ads should ensure, if you follow them, that your advertising is effective. Advertising is a huge subject, and there is plenty more which could be said about it if there were room to say it. If you feel that advertising is a large part of your particular line of work, and you would like to know more about it, I recommend that you read more on the subject. *Teach Yourself Marketing Your Small Business*, also in this series, contains a whole chapter on the subject, virtually all of which will be relevant to you as a freelance.

Approaching prospects

Getting your prospects to come to you is often the best method of making contact, as we've seen, but it is always preferable for you to go to them if you can – it is a better guarantee that the contact will actually be made. As we've seen, you have to know who they are in order to do this.

The crucial thing to remember as a freelance is that when you do persuade someone to give you work, they will feel they are buying *your time*, not just the services you offer. As we've seen, that is part of what freelancing is about: your clients want to employ you personally because they trust you and they want the personal skills you offer. So your relationships with your clients are personal ones.

Often you find that you have clients who you speak to so often that you end up knowing where they live, what their children's names are, and discussing the ups and downs of their Christmas or why the dinner party they went to last night resulted in the awful headache they have right now. It's far from unusual in many lines of freelance work for some clients to end up as personal friends.

All of this should influence the way you approach new prospects. I'm not suggesting you start your letters to them 'Hello, you old buffer', but you should approach them in a way which assumes that if they offer you work a friendly relationship will develop. Make them feel that your approach to them is a one-off, personal one. You saw an article about their company's recent growth in the paper, for example, and thought they might be interested in using a marketing consultant to help them cope positively with all the changes that growth can generate.

It may be that you saw similar articles about five other companies and you've sent all their MDs the same letter. But they should feel the letter is personal, because if they want to use a freelance, they will expect that kind of service from them.

The initial approach

There are generally two ways of initiating contact: by phone or by letter. However, you should bear in mind from the start that with almost any freelance job you will need a meeting with the prospect before they commit themselves to using you – and you sometimes need much more, in the way of proposals, meetings with other key personnel and so on. So the aim of any call or letter is not to get the work itself, but simply to get an appointment.

So you aren't asking the letter or call to do the impossible. It has to persuade the prospect only that it is worth talking to you about what you do. They aren't expected to commit themselves yet. For this reason, you don't want to give them enough information to decide against using you. You want them to delay the decision until after you've met. You want to give them only enough information about what you do to decide that it's worth getting together.

This doesn't mean being secretive – that would be counter-productive. But a letter can be very simple (using the same principle as for advertising, or stressing the benefit to the prospect), such as the example shown in Figure 9.1.

Dear Mrs Boothroyd

I gather that you don't employ a secretary, but perhaps you sometimes wish you did? Just because you don't regularly have enough work to justify a secretary doesn't mean there aren't times when the typing or photocopying piles up.

I'm a fully qualified freelance secretary, with fifteen years' experience in shorthand, typing and other secretarial skills. If you occasionally need to find someone who can take these tasks off your hands, I can help.

Perhaps it might be worth our meeting up to discuss whether I can do anything for you. I'll give you a ring in the next few days, to see if we can arrange something.

Yours sincerely

Figure 9.1 Sample letter of approach to a prospective client

The example in Figure 9.1 demonstrates the most important points about writing letters to prospects:

- The style is personal and friendly without being too informal.
- The letter is addressed to the prospect by name.
- The tone is not a pushy, hard-sell one.
- The letter gives the information necessary so the prospect can decide whether a meeting would be useful. It doesn't give the kind of detail you would want to save for a meeting – and which the prospect will want to find out if the letter kindles their interest – such as how fast you work, what rate you charge, whether you collect and deliver the work, and so on.
- It leaves the ball in your court. If you finish by asking a prospect to contact you, and they don't, you are a bit lost for a follow-up. So always give yourself a reason to call them.

In fact, this letter should follow the same rules – AIDA – as the advertisements we just looked at, only in a far more personal, informal way. It should attract the reader's attention, stimulate their interest, create a desire for your services, and specify the action to take – in this case, do nothing and await your phone call.

Once you have given the letter time to arrive, and a day or two for your prospect to read it, make the promised phone call. Don't put it off for too long or they have time to forget the letter. I would suggest a week: if you have set aside, for example, Monday afternoons for finding new work, send out the letter one Monday and phone the following Monday.

When you phone, the first thing you will do is to introduce yourself and say something along the lines of 'I hope you received the letter I sent you last week?' Then ask a question to ascertain whether they might be interested in your services. But don't ask a closed question – one which can be answered with a yes or no. If you ask 'Do you have a lot of typing to do?', and they say 'No', it makes the conversation difficult to pursue. So prepare a question to which they have to give a fuller answer, such as 'How much time do you spend typing in an average week?'

Anyone who wants to be obstructive and difficult can refuse to answer almost any question – but then they were probably never going to become a client anyway. What you're trying to do is to open up a conversation with anyone who is a genuine potential client, and open questions – which require fuller answers – are the way to do this.

Once you have established a level of interest from the prospect, ask if you could meet them to talk further about what you do. If they start asking you a lot of questions, don't let them find out everything on the phone or they won't need the meeting. If they end up using you, that's fine. But if their final decision is *not* to use you, there's a chance that a personal meeting would have shifted the balance the other way. So if they start pumping you for prices and specifics, that's the time to say 'You know, I wonder if it would make more sense to meet up and I can bring along some samples of my work and we can go through the details. Why don't we fix up a time for me to visit you next week?'

Face-to-face contacts

The most common initial contacts other than by phone or letter are contacts you make face to face. This can happen at trade fairs and business events, or even at social occasions when you meet people through mutual friends. The best way to handle these is to make sure you always have a few business cards with you – even when you're out visiting friends.

A face-to-face conversation can lead directly to an appointment to discuss work, which is great if it happens. But often things don't get that far because the situation isn't right. At a friend's dinner party, for example, it would be a little rude to buttonhole one of the other guests and start touting for work. At a trade fair, exhibitors often have prospects at the stand and don't want to spend long talking to you. So give them a business card (we'll look at what should be on your business card in the next chapter). If you can, get your prospects' card, or jot down their name and phone number, and call them in the next few days to fix up a meeting.

You don't have to ask for business

There is one other technique which can work very well in many lines of work. Sometimes you find it difficult to get people to arrange to see you, and often the reason is because people have no work at the moment and don't want to have to say 'no' to your face. The problem is that when they do reach a point when they might use your services, you won't have had the chance to sell yourself to them.

Most people dislike saying no – they'd rather not say no over the phone to arranging a meeting, but it beats saying no to giving you work once you're sitting across the desk from them.

If this happens to you frequently, try a different tack. Write to your prospects saying that you don't expect them to have any work at the moment, but you are just setting out as a freelance and you'd be very grateful for their advice on what kind of services would be most useful, and what sort of price they would expect to pay, if ever they did have need of a freelance in your field.

What you are saying, in effect, is that if they meet with you they won't have to say no because you won't be asking for work. And stick to this. If they agree to meet you, don't ask. Just give them enough information so that they make a mental note that you're just what they need if ever they *do* want a freelance media buyer, customer relations trainer, dressmaker or whatever you do. And give them a business card, of course – you can't give away too many business cards.

This approach can work very well; not only are people relieved by not having to turn you down, but they are also flattered that you want their advice – a combination that will persuade many of them to see you.

The sales conversation

Once you've successfully set up a meeting with your prospect, how do you handle it to ensure that by the time you emerge the prospect has been converted into a new client? There are several guidelines to follow, which we'll look at in a moment, but broadly speaking the conversation should take the following format:

- opening pleasantries
- you ask questions to establish what would be needed from you (during which time the prospect does the vast majority of the talking)
- you expand on what you can do for the prospect
- you close the sale.

In order to do this, there are certain important guidelines to follow. Once you have learnt them, you will find that selling is really very simple. You don't need to be a pushy salesperson to get work; in freelancing it is absolutely the wrong approach. You are going for a friendly, personal, soft sell approach. If your prospects are genuinely potential clients, a simple explanation of what you do, expressed in the right way, will clinch the sale. So what is the right way?

Listen

For a start, you need to be a good listener. Not only should you let the prospect do most of the talking, especially at the start, but you should appear interested in what is being said to you. Your job is to guide the prospect into talking about the things you need to know about. As well as providing you with the information you need, this will also give the prospect the impression that you are interested in his or her situation and that you want to help – rather than simply wanting to get some work.

Start by asking broad, general questions which give you a clear idea of what the business is about and how it works, or when the wedding is and how long the couple have known each other, or what their taste in gardening is and how they've coped in the garden up to now. You're showing interest and painting the background to the work you hope to win from them. So part of the aim is to create a rapport and make them feel they'd like to work with you, and part of it is to establish facts which may be useful later on; you'll have a hard time designing an effective computer program for a company if you don't know how they work, how many departments there are and how they interrelate. If you're hoping to arrange a wedding for a couple, you want a picture of their style and taste in order to be able to come up with ideas which they feel are in keeping with their own views.

Once you have a background picture, start asking them more specific questions about the work they might want you to do. If they think they want you to produce a sales brochure, ask them who it's targeted at, what their budget for it is, and so on. If they want you to make a dress for them, what style did they have in mind and when are they planning to wear it? If you're a researcher, what is the subject of the research, why do they want it done, do they want you to present conclusions or merely information, and when do they need it done by?

Discuss benefits, not features

The prospect should be doing most of the talking for the first three-quarters or so of the meeting, guided by your questions. Once you have all the information you need, you can start to explain how you can be of help. It is critical, as in the advertising techniques we looked at earlier, that you talk in terms of the benefits to the prospect.

As a media buyer, for example, don't bore prospects with the minute details of how you do your job – if they found it interesting they'd do it themselves instead of hiring you – just tell them how much hassle you're saving them, and how your expertise as a media buyer will get them much better deals than they would otherwise get.

If you're a journalist, let the newspaper or magazine know that your background in their particular field means you can turn out really good stories. If you're talking to a racing car magazine about covering a particular motor show, let them know that three years as a top rally driver means that you really understand racing cars from an enthusiast's point of view.

Of course you should explain the mechanics of your job if they want to know, but any selling, or persuading, you do successfully will be achieved by demonstrating to prospects how they will benefit from putting work out to you.

Reassure the prospect

If you are listening well, you should be able to tell if your prospect has any worries. If you are repeatedly questioned about the cost, or ways of keeping it down, be as reassuring as you can. Or prospects may seem worried that your standards aren't as high as theirs – if they take you on in the garden, are you going to weed up their prize verbascums thinking they're dandelions? Offer to give them references to follow up.

Whatever their concerns, you should be able to reassure them if you are listening carefully. And if you think there's something they're not saying, ask: 'I get the feeling you're still concerned about something. Can you tell me what's worrying you?'

By the time you have reached the end of the sales interview, you should have identified all the prospect's worries and provided reassurance on each point. After that, the only place to go is for you to close the sale.

Don't force a sale

If you know anything about professional selling, you will know that there are hundreds of techniques for closing the sale: the alternative close, the puppydog close, the assumptive close, and so on. But they are all sophisticated versions of the same thing – asking for an order.

There's no point trying to push prospects to give you work if they don't want to – you'll simply ensure that they are put off giving you work if ever they have any in future. In the personal, friendly atmosphere of a conversation with a freelance, your prospects may well offer you work without your having to ask. But life isn't always that easy, and sometimes they resist offering because they are waiting for you to ask.

So ask. It's very simple. Wait until you feel all the useful information there is has been exchanged and your prospect is in a position to make a decision. Then simply say 'Do you have any work at the moment that I can do?' Or 'I'm free to start in the garden the week after next. Would you like me to book you in?'

Keeping your clients

Finding prospects and turning them into clients can be time consuming, and it occupies time which you would rather occupy earning money. Once you have all the clients you need, you can cut right back on recruiting new ones, and spend your time earning instead. You still need to be on the lookout for new prospects, in case you lose any of your current clients, but it becomes a much lower priority.

The high priority, now, is keeping the clients you've got. You will always lose a few – they go bust, they get bought out and an edict comes down that they are to cut back on using freelances, your contact moves on and their replacement has their own list of freelances which doesn't include you, and so on.

But a lot of freelances lose work for the wrong reasons – because their clients aren't that bothered about using them and switch to someone else as soon as a competitor approaches them. Your clients will stop using you if you give them any excuse to, so don't. Make sure that no competitor could offer anything that you can't do better. Your clients need to be confident that:

- you are always friendly and helpful
- you always charge a fair price, and you don't increase it without discussing it with them first
- you always deliver on time
- your work is consistently of a very high standard
- you are entirely trustworthy when it comes to keeping confidential information to yourself.

If all of these things are always true, it will be hard for any competitor to persuade your clients to use them instead.

And on top of all that, you need to go a little bit further. You have a relationship with your clients, and all relationships need some effort to keep them operating smoothly. If either of you feels taken for granted, things can turn sour. So make your clients feel valued, as we saw in Chapter 5. Contact them after an important job to make sure they were happy with the work. Take your grade one clients out for lunch, or at least a lunchtime drink, once or twice a year just to discuss whether there is anything you could be doing differently for them – or any other work that they want to put out and which you could help with.

Send them a Christmas card, wish them luck with their driving test, ask on the phone if they had a good holiday. Sound as though they matter to you – they do. Time invested in keeping your clients once you have won them can only be time well spent. Anything which minimises all that expensive, unpaid time recruiting new clients has to be worth it.

Summary

- It is important to have the right number of clients. Categorise your clients according to the grading system described in this chapter.

- Select suitable prospects. These could include your former employer.

- Be prepared to sell your services, by placing advertisements and by making approaches.

- Finding prospects and turning them into clients can be time consuming, so make sure you keep your clients once you have won them.

10 YOUR PERSONAL IMAGE

As a freelance you are effectively selling yourself, so the way you come across to clients and potential clients is all important. This means your manner, your style of dress, your car, your business cards, your letter writing style, your time-keeping – all of these must present a consistent and professional image. It doesn't have to cost you any more than presenting a poor image; it just takes an awareness of how you come across to your clients. This chapter is all about the areas where you can unwittingly send out the wrong signals, and explains how to make sure you impress every time.

Your personal manner

We've already discussed the fact that your clients are employing you personally to do the work, because they like and trust you, and want access to your skills or expertise. Presenting a friendly and helpful attitude is obviously important in any business, but it is especially so when you are a freelance. If your clients decide they don't like you, or that your manner makes them feel unimportant, belittled or taken for granted, they will probably stop giving you work.

So a friendly approach is important – and important all the time. When you speak to your clients – face to face or on the phone – smile and be friendly, ask if they had a good weekend, make sure they enjoy the conversation, however brief. Some of your clients may be particularly dense when it comes to understanding what you need to do the job, or they may be hopelessly unorganised and always give you work at the last minute, or perhaps they can't see why a particular request is time consuming or expensive for you to fulfil.

However impossible they may be, never let your clients see that you think they are stupid or hopeless. If you need to discuss the problem with them, don't criticise. You could say to a disorganised client, for example: 'I know you're terribly busy and it's not easy for you to see in advance when the work is going to arise. But the problem is that if I don't have enough notice of a job it creates extra work for me trying to fit it in. Sooner or later I'm going to have to increase my fees to cover the cost of the extra work – unless we can find a way to book the work in further ahead.'

This is a much friendlier approach than saying 'Look, you're going to have to try thinking ahead occasionally, or I'm going to have to put my prices up.' The first approach has at least as much chance of working, and it hasn't made your client feel put down or defensive.

Following through the friendly approach

Most freelances have a good personal manner when they speak to their clients, or they learn it pretty fast . . . or they go out of business. But what about the times you communicate with your clients without speaking directly to them? One of the key points about your image is that it should be consistent. It's extremely difficult to promote a friendly, professional image if any part of your behaviour contradicts the rest.

To give you an example, your outgoing answerphone message needs to be friendly and helpful. If it is brusque or sounds inefficient, you will have to work twice as hard at other aspects of your image to counteract this impression. Your message should give your name and your phone number, or at least the last part of it, and apologise for not being there in person. Say something like: 'Hello. You're through to Robin Smith on 654321. I'm sorry there's no one here to take your call at the moment, but if you'd like to leave a message after the tone, I'll get back to you as soon as I can. Thanks for calling.'

Likewise, if you leave a message for your client on an answerphone or voice mail, it should sound pleasant and friendly. Smile as you speak – they can hear it when they play the message back later. You may be one of the millions of people who hate leaving messages; in this case, before you lift the phone up rehearse what you are going to say if you get an answerphone. You'll find that you soon get used to using the things, even if you never learn to enjoy it.

Written communications are another opportunity to be friendly. Make sure your letters are friendly, and take the trouble to add a compliments slip to your invoices – it's just that bit friendlier. You can simply sign your name without adding any message.

Your dress sense

I can't tell you what to wear; it depends on your job. The question is, how will your clients expect you to dress? If you are a business consultant, you should wear a suit and tie if you're a man, and a smart business outfit if you're a woman. You may feel that in your line of work other dress codes apply – designers can usually get away with looking a bit arty, journalists can probably get away with almost anything.

Dressmakers need to be well dressed to give confidence in their skills. Gardeners might dress smartly for an appointment at which they aren't expected to get dirty, but should look as if they are happy to get stuck in. If they turned up with perfectly manicured and polished nails, an expensive hairdo, lots of fancy jewellery and a pair of stilettos, the prospect might feel that they just didn't seem the gardening type.

So look at it from your clients' perspective. What will they expect of you? Then make sure you give them what they want. But whatever your line of work, you should be clean and well turned out in your personal choice of clothing, shoes, make-up, jewellery and all the rest of it. And don't forget all the rest of it – if you're wearing a smart business outfit with shiny shoes and a sensible haircut, don't carry a grubby, tatty old briefcase which should have been thrown in the dustbin years ago. You should consider your style in terms of:

- clothes (including your overcoat, hat, gloves and anything else you remove when you arrive)
- shoes
- jewellery
- hairstyle
- make-up
- bag or briefcase.

Your car

The car you drive says a great deal about you, and needs some thought. If you're a forestry adviser, you probably need a tough, four-wheel drive vehicle. As a PR, on the other hand, a smart saloon might be better. You should also bear in mind what the cost of your car implies about your earnings. Your clients want you to look successful, but they don't want to feel they're paying through the nose just so you can drive the luxury car of your dreams. They will feel they've paid for your car, and in a sense they're right. So what would they want you to drive?

As a broad rule of thumb, it's not a bad idea to drive a car which is about one step down the ladder from your clients' car. Being one unit of snob value below them makes your clients feel that *they* are employing *you*, but it puts you close enough to them that they feel you are on their wavelength.

If you work as a board level consultant for big organisations whose directors – your clients – all drive Rolls Royces and Bentleys, you should probably drive, say, a Mercedes. If you're a private music teacher whose pupils' parents all drive Range Rovers, perhaps you should drive a middle range Volvo or Peugeot.

Whatever you drive, it should always appear well looked after. Keep it clean – put it through the car wash regularly. Repair any scratches or bumps promptly, and make sure there aren't any obvious defects such as a headlight out.

Your image on paper

We've already looked at the need to employ a friendly manner in your written communications, but it's equally important to come across as being smart and professional. There can be a risk for freelances that because they work from home and aren't running a business, clients may see them as less professional than those of their competitors who work from offices. Any danger of this attitude in your clients can be dispelled, but only if you are consistently professional in your approach so that there is no room for doubt in their minds.

When it comes to letters, make sure they are laid out well, with the recipient's name and address typed at the top left, with the date underneath. Don't cram the text up at the top of the page; spread it out or move it into the middle of the page so that it looks more attractive. Any other typed material, such as invoices, schedules and so on should also be laid out smartly. Type your letters, and sign your name in ink at the bottom. You can hand write compliments slips, but if your writing is atrocious it would be better to type them.

Make sure that you give a professional impression by using accurate punctuation and spelling. If you can't spell or punctuate, get your computer or a friend or relative to check your letters for you. You should find that most of the hard-to-spell words you use crop up regularly, so learn these ones – or at least write them out and keep them pinned up by your desk to refer to.

Stationery

You will need to have letterheads in order to give a professional look to your letters. You can set these up on a template on your computer, or you can have them specially printed. If your letterhead is on the computer it will be reproduced in black by your desktop printer (unless you have some really fancy equipment). This is fine, but if you don't want black (and don't have fancy equipment) you will need to pay a printer to produce your letterheads for you.

Going to a printer can be the sensible option because you can get compliments slips, letterheads and business cards printed at the same time. As a freelance, these are probably the only three pieces of stationery you need, although you may choose to have something else such as invoices printed as well. I would recommend compliments slips because they are extremely useful if you just want to write a brief note to accompany an invoice, a report or a manuscript.

As a freelance, you don't need a fancy letterhead. Just your name, address and contact numbers (phone, fax, e-mail) will do fine. However, you might like to add a very simple graphic to this which illustrates what you do in some way; it can help to fix you in prospects' minds and help your clients recognise your letterheads. If you are a writer, you could underline your name with a simple design of a pen; a tailor could have a needle and thread logo; a violin teacher could have a violin bow or a violin, and so on.

If you are having your letterheads, compliments slips and business cards printed, you might as well use a colour other than black. It's more distinctive and the extra printing cost is minimal. Think about the psychological impact of different colours and choose one that suits your work.

- Deep, rich colours such as sea greens and burgundies imply traditional quality and might suit a business consultant.
- Bright colours are fun and modern and would give an appropriate impression for a children's party organiser.

- Brown and grass green are rustic and would suit a gardener, although a very upmarket gardener might be better off with a colour like terracotta which has more class to it.
- Pastels are quite feminine and probably better for a wedding organiser or a dressmaker.
- Grey and blue are very professional colours; good for a media buyer or a researcher.

Business cards

Business cards are a terrific way of getting new business. The reason is that most people seem unable to throw them away. They keep them in little boxes or in the bottom drawer of their desk, and every time they look for one of them in the pile, their eye skims over all the others. So when, a year later, they need a software engineer, they know they have a business card somewhere and they dig it out.

For this reason, you should distribute your business cards as widely as you can. Clip them to the letters you send to prospects, because even if they say no to you now, they may want your services in a few months time. Hand them out to anyone who can possibly want them, especially – as we saw earlier – to people you meet in social situations where it would be bad form to start selling to them on the spot.

Your professionalism

Everything you do should reinforce your image of being friendly and professional. Always turn up to meetings on time, and make sure you have all the papers you need with you. There's nothing worse than arriving ten minutes late and then spending the next five minutes leafing through papers until you find the right one or – worse – discovering you've left it behind. The client is likely to think 'If they can't take care of themselves, what sort of care are they going to take over *my* work?'

The key is to take time – schedule it if necessary – to think through meetings in advance and prepare everything you need. Check train times or make sure you have enough petrol in the car; don't leave these things to the last minute. If you know you're a waste of space in the mornings, get everything organised the night before if you have a morning appointment.

Always meet deadlines. Your clients don't want excuses; they want the work you're supposed to have finished. Missing deadlines is one of the fastest ways to persuade your clients to look elsewhere for someone more reliable to give their work to. And invoice promptly, too. Late invoices may sometimes give clients a welcome breathing space, but even so they look unprofessional. Once again, your clients need to know that you look after your own work professionally in order to be confident that you will apply the same standards to the work you do for them.

And whatever you do, don't make the classic mistake of failing at your own skill. Make certain that you aren't a typist whose letters contain spelling mistakes, a book-keeper who forgets to send out invoices, a time management consultant who arrives late for meetings or an image consultant whose car is badly in need of a wash.

So maintain the highest possible standards and project a consistently reliable, smart and professional image:

■ never deliver work after the agreed deadline
■ always deliver work to a professional standard, and presented smartly
■ always arrive on time for appointments
■ always have the right papers with you and know where to find them
■ make the effort to remember people's names
■ if you promise a phone call, make it at the agreed time
■ if you say you'll put something in the post, do it
■ invoice on time
■ don't fail at your own skill.

If you can project an image that is consistently friendly and professional, you will go a long way to impressing your prospects and clients, and ensuring that it takes a lot for them even to consider switching their allegiance to one of your competitors.

CASE STUDY: PROJECTING THE RIGHT IMAGE ON THE PHONE

Belinda Faulkner was a book-keeper. She looked after other people's accounts on her own computer at home. Her clients needed to have a great deal of trust in her; she not only had access to their private financial details, she also needed to do the work very accurately or they could be in a lot of trouble.

Belinda had two teenage children who, like most teenagers, spent a lot of time on the phone. Belinda restricted them to making calls after 5.30 and at weekends, but they used to answer the phone if it rang, especially if Belinda was out. This should have been helpful, but Belinda's children weren't used to talking to clients. Their manner was pleasant but rather offhand, and the disappointment that the call wasn't from one of their friends often showed in their voices. What's more, they often forgot to pass on messages.

A few of Belinda's clients thought the children were part-time helpers, and weren't impressed. They told Belinda, and she realised that the impression her children gave over the phone didn't suit her work. So she did two things: she installed an answerphone, and she gave her children a lesson in how to answer the phone professionally. Then she explained to them that she would be grateful if they would answer the phone if they were going to be efficient and friendly, but if they weren't in the mood, they should leave the call for the answerphone rather than answer the call badly. After that, Belinda didn't receive any more complaints, and her children became rather proud of their own proficiency at answering the phone well.

Summary

- As a freelance you are effectively selling yourself, so the way you come across to clients and potential clients is all important.
- Your image includes your style of dress, your car, your business cards, your letter writing skill, your time-keeping and so on. These should be appropriate for the business you are in and be seen as such by your clients and potential clients.
- Everything you do should reinforce your image of being friendly and professional.

11 | WRITING PROPOSALS

Not every freelance needs to write proposals, but an enormous number get most of their work this way. If you're a writer, software engineer, researcher, PR, film director, trainer, computer programmer, media buyer or designer, or in any other line of freelance work where your clients are business ones, you will probably have to write a proposal sooner or later.

Many freelances start out with no experience at all of proposal writing and then find it is their only means of getting much, if not all, of their work. If you are one of these, the good news is that persuasive and professional proposals really aren't difficult to put together; you just have to know the rules.

What is a proposal?

The first time you are ever asked for a proposal, it can be unnerving. 'Can you put a proposal in the post to me?' asks your client. 'Sure, no problem' you reply. 'You'll have it next week.' You put the phone down, or leave the room, and think to yourself: 'Help! What's a proposal? What should it say? How long should it be? What should it look like?' You know it's some kind of sales document designed to persuade your prospect or client to give you a particular job. But that's as far as most people's knowledge goes until they have to write one themselves.

You probably know more than you think you do. A proposal is precisely that: a few pages of persuasive writing which will convince the reader that you're the best person for the job. You could impart the same information by having a sales conversation with the client, but a proposal has additional benefits for both of you:

■ It gets the proposed work down in writing so you both know what you are – and are not – proposing to do for your client.

- As it is in writing, there can be no argument later when the client thinks you were going to do something that you didn't think you were supposed to do, such as give a detailed list of all your research sources, when you expected to deliver only the findings of your research.

- It can establish your legal rights if there is a copyright element (if this is important check with a solicitor precisely how to establish your rights).

- Since it is a printed document, it can be circulated to anyone who needs to see it, who may not have been present at a sales meeting.

- It focuses both your minds clearly, so you can think through any problems at this stage, such as a difference between you and your client over the precise objective of the work, and sort them out before you agree the commission.

Your proposal should contain everything your client needs to make a decision on whether to give you the work, including everything you want the client to know because you think it will help persuade them. Often, your client will have asked for proposals from one or two of your competitors as well, so this is your chance to show that you're the most professional and well presented, as well as the one offering the best work.

The rest of this chapter is about how to put together these few pages to gain the maximum impact. You need to be clear about what you're doing before you start, collect together all the information you need, structure it in the most helpful way for your client, and make sure it looks good and contains all the information they need.

This chapter is all you need to put together a professional proposal, whatever your line of work. However, if your clients regularly ask for proposals from prospective suppliers, it's not a bad idea to ask them to show you one or two. You probably don't want to tell them you haven't a clue what you're doing, but you could say that since you have never written a proposal for *them* before, you think it might help to see an example or two of the kind of proposal they particularly like to receive, to give you an idea of length, depth, layout and so on. You'll manage fine without, but it might give you more confidence if you have a couple of good examples in front of you.

What a proposal is not

A proposal explains what you intend to do if given the job, and how you will do it. However, it is not a draft contract. As we saw in Chapter 6, one of the rules of negotiating is not to promise anything until you know all the facts, and know exactly what the client wants in terms of price, delivery times and so on. So a proposal shouldn't commit you to any of these bargaining points.

Suppose you are a PR submitting a proposal for a one-year contract. You would set out what level of work you could offer: half a day a week, three major events organised during the year, press clippings collected and so on. But the proposal is not the place to start negotiating. So don't use it to discuss:

- fees
- terms of payment
- delivery dates
- expenses arrangements
- client support (if it's negotiable)

. . . or any other negotiable elements. These can all be saved until later. Sometimes your client will ask you to give a price, or commit yourself to some other negotiable detail, when you submit your proposal. If you feel you really can't argue about this – perhaps the client needs to compare your prices with other people's – at least don't commit yourself. Give the figure but say something like: 'The exact fee will depend on several factors, such as the number of people to be trained, the training venue, the precise length of the training session and the nature of the handout material. But as a guide, a ball park figure might be in the region of £3,500.' It is often a good idea to keep this information separate from the proposal by putting it in a covering letter, still making it clear that it's subject to discussion.

Bear in mind that when you do come to negotiate, your client may try to beat you down on the price you have written down, and will strongly resist your pushing it up. So give a high enough price that you have some room to drop it if you have to. This is difficult if you are in competition for the work, but you will simply have to judge what you can afford and how much you want the work.

The alternative approach is to agree with the client that the fee will *not* be negotiable. So if your proposal is accepted, the client can't start haggling over the price. This makes your life a little easier, but what happens if the client agrees the fixed price and then tries to double the workload? If you go for this option, spell out exactly what the price includes so there can be no justification for the client trying to get more for the money. These warnings should illustrate why it is far better to avoid mentioning negotiable factors such as price at all at the proposal stage. Otherwise you're really into the whole area of giving quotes, which has nothing to do with presenting proposals.

Setting your objective

The first thing you need to do before you start working on the proposal is to identify your objective and write it down. It should take the form of a single sentence, or possibly two sentences, which express clearly the purpose of the proposal. The point of this exercise is:

- ■ *to help you decide what information to include or leave out of the proposal*: The objective you write down will function as a touchstone against which you can measure all the information you collect. If it doesn't fall within the boundaries of the objective, you should leave it out.

- ■ *to help you pitch the proposal suitably*: In order to persuade your client to accept your proposal, you will need to express what you have to say from the client's perspective, and highlight the benefits of accepting it. Your objective will help you to view the subject from the client's point of view.

- ■ *to help you establish a clear brief*: The objective expresses clearly what the proposal is for. Once you have written it down you can see whether you have described exactly what the client wants from you. If you are unsure, this is your chance to call the client and clarify the brief. One of the biggest potential pitfalls with proposal writing is that you will write the 'wrong' proposal. This happens if the idea inside your mind is different from the one inside your client's mind. Setting an objective, and agreeing it with your client if there is any danger of confusion, is the best way to prevent this happening.

- ■ *to help you write the report more easily*: It's always easier to do anything if you have a clear idea of what you are aiming to achieve. You will find that having established your objective, the whole process of writing the proposal is quicker and easier.

Wording the objective

The objective needs to be specific in order to be useful. Obviously the objective of any sales proposal is to persuade clients that the services you offer meet their requirements. But you want an objective which doesn't apply to any proposal – an objective which is particular to this proposal. As a PR, your objective might be: 'to persuade the client that you can raise the profile of the business'. This is certainly your aim, but it doesn't cover all of it.

You still need to incorporate the benefits to the client. Let's imagine that the client is working within a fairly tight budget; you would need to mention this. And perhaps the client has (or you feel needs to have) a clear picture of what it wants the profile-raising to achieve for it – otherwise the client won't know whether it has worked or not. Here's a more specific objective: 'to persuade the client that you can raise the positive profile of the business cost-effectively, so that attendance at the client's trade show stands increases by at least 50 per cent'.

That's the kind of objective you're after. It's specific, it tells you exactly what to concentrate on, and it keeps you focused on the benefits the client is looking for.

Using your objective

There is no point in setting an objective if you write it down and then forget it, and shove the piece of paper under the bottom of a pile of other papers. An objective is a working tool to enable you to write a clear, focused proposal; so use it.

The objective should sit on your desk in front of you while you are writing the proposal, and you should keep referring to it to make sure you are following it. It should keep your mind firmly fixed on the benefits to the client, and it will help you decide what information to include and what information is irrelevant to the purpose of the proposal.

Collecting the information

You will almost always need to gather information you don't already have in order to write a sales proposal. There are three main categories of information you are likely to need:

- information about the client
- information about what you can offer
- information to back up your case.

Information about the client

You can't tailor your services to fit the client if you don't have the measure of them. In general, you need to know what the company does and how, how it is structured and so on. If you're a PR, for example, you also need to know what PR activity the client currently engages in, how effective it is, what events they run, how the events are organised and publicised, how many press releases they send out and when, and so on.

You can get most of this information from the client who wants you to write a good proposal and hopefully do the work needed and so will recognise that you need to know these things. Ask for copies of annual reports, brochures, customer newsletters, past press clippings and so on. And if necessary, ask to arrange a meeting where you can be briefed on anything you can't find out from these other documents. You may also need to look elsewhere for some information. In the case of PR, you might want to find out the outsider's view of the organisation, to see what the PR is *really* like. You might call up your local paper's business editor (who, as a PR, you will know) and get an opinion. Or ask some of your client's suppliers (you will be very discreet, of course).

If you're a freelance trainer, you might want an outside opinion on the company's customer relations image; as a computer programmer you might want to talk to other similar companies to your clients and find out what kind of system they find best. As a consultant you might want to find copies of previously published articles about the company. So whatever your line of work, you may want to supplement the information your client gives you.

Information about what you can offer

Of course you know much of this already. You know your own skills and capabilities, in terms of both expertise and your available time. But you might need to check with your own suppliers whether you can get what you need from them. If your client wanted you to publicise events by mailing a particular group of people, could you get hold of a suitable mailing list that was up to date and within your client's budget? If you're a print buyer and your client wants all the brochures and sales material to be printed on card in the cut-out shape of an elephant, can you find someone to do this?

Information to back up your case

The final category of information is designed to persuade your client that what you propose is the best option for them. You might want to track down case studies or research, or technical information, to lend weight to your arguments. For example, as a marketing consultant proposing to co-ordinate a direct mail campaign, you might want to find research which supports your case that it is more cost effective to pay extra for a mailing list that has contact names on it than to use a cheaper list which doesn't.

Each piece of information you collect should contribute to the objective you have set yourself. Having specified in your objective that, for example, you will achieve the target working to a tight budget, there is no point in spending half a day researching a product your client cannot possibly afford. As a wedding organiser, you would be wasting your time checking whether you can find a supplier who can hire you 150 reproduction Louis XV chairs, if your clients have specified that their budget is fairly tight.

Organising the information

Once you have collected everything together, the next step is to organise it. The way to do this is to write down each piece of information – everything you want to say – on a separate slip of paper. If there is a lengthy chunk of information in one of your books or brochures, don't bother writing it all out; just write yourself a note on one of your slips of paper to remind you of the gist of it, and add a note reminding you where to find it.

At the end of this process, you have a desk covered in little pieces of paper, each with a piece of information on it. The final step in collecting your information together is to sort these slips of paper into logical groups. Only you know what these groups are, and there may be more than one choice of groupings. That's fine; just pick the one you feel happiest with. The point of the exercise is threefold:

- it is invaluable in helping you focus your mind on the subject
- it gives you a chance to double check each piece of

information against the objective, and to make sure you aren't repeating points

■ it ensures that related pieces of information are kept together so that each individual item is much less likely to be omitted by mistake, or only found after you've finished the report.

Although these groups are not the final structure for the report – as we're about to see – they will probably be incorporated into the final structure. Assuming this happens, as it generally does, you will find that this process has saved you a lot of time later on.

Structuring the proposal

A good report should have a beginning, a middle and an end. This makes it easier to write and easier to read. Readability is very important; your client often isn't nearly as bothered as you whether the proposal is effective. They don't necessarily want to make the effort if it's hard going. They'd be just as happy to commission your competitor if their proposal is easier to read. So it's important you make it as easy and enjoyable as possible for your client to read.

There is a simple formula to follow when you write a proposal; you could call it the three Ps:

■ Position (the current arrangement)
■ Problem (the reason why it needs to change)
■ Proposal (what can be done about it).

As a PR, you might say that the *position* is that the client currently has no formal PR arrangements at all; the *problem* is that very few of their prospects have heard of them, so they have to approach new customers cold instead of 'warm'; and the *proposal* is that they pay you a retainer to spend half a day a week raising their profile.

Sometimes there is more than one option for resolving the problem. Maybe you could spend half a day a fortnight simply getting out four press releases a month. Or you could put in half a day a week to keep them in the press and organise three major events a year. Or you could spend a day and a half a week looking after press releases, revamping their corporate image, and organising an event a month to promote them.

In this case, you will want to outline the various options, or possibilities, and then go on to propose the one that most accurately fits the objective you worked out, in terms of the cost, the level of profile-raising the client wants, or any other benefits you set out. When you have more than one approach to suggest, the formula is upgraded to the four Ps:

- Position (the current arrangement)
- Problem (why it needs to change)
- Possibilities (the options for resolving it)
- Proposal (your recommended solution).

Position

Stating the position may not take long – usually anything from a paragraph to a page at the very most – but it is important. You need to state simply what the current position is. As a PR, summarise the company's current PR activities and their level of success. If you are a trainer, outline the current training arrangements in the client's company or department. As a computer consultant, state what system the company uses at the moment.

A proposal is a bit like a journey – with a beginning, a middle and an end. You and your readers are setting out to explore the problem and discover a solution to it. Stating the position is a way of identifying the starting point for the journey.

You need to outline the starting point for several reasons:

- It ensures that everyone is starting from the same point, and establishes what that point is. Your client might think they are doing a rather good job of their PR at the moment, although they'd like to do even better. You might think their present performance is atrocious. Writing down the current position means that you are all setting out together on your journey of exploration.

- It gives you a chance to show that you understand the background to the situation, which makes the rest of your proposal more credible.

- It establishes all the facts which the readers will need to know in order to make sense of the rest of the proposal. If the proposal is a journey, this process is like checking the contents of everyone's kitbag to make sure they have all the equipment they need.

- It enables you to fill in the facts for the readers who don't know them without patronising the ones who do. If you are submitting a proposal to the marketing director, that doesn't mean no one else will read it. It might be circulated to the entire board before your contact decides whether to give you the work. And some of the directors may be very out of touch with the company's marketing activity.

Problem

This next section of the proposal, which again may be anything from a paragraph to a page (rarely longer), explains why the present arrangement needs to change. It may be because it creates problems, or it may be because it misses an opportunity. The current level of PR activity might be fine – the company's image may be very good among those who know of it – except that there is a potential for a far higher public awareness which is being missed.

Your aim is to make sure, by the end of this section, that the reader is left with the feeling that things have got to change. Something must be done. Now you are merely left with the job of persuading them that your solution is the best.

Possibilities

If you have a range of possibilities to cover, this is the place to do it, and it should be the longest section of the proposal. However, it should still be only a few pages at most – a good proposal rarely has more than ten or a dozen pages at most, and many very good proposals are only two or three pages long. As we will see later, you can always put non-essential but useful information in an appendix. Brevity is an excellent quality in a proposal – your client doesn't want to waste unnecessary time reading it. Make sure you include all the information the reader needs – and no more.

Start by putting the case for the broad approach you propose. Obviously, as a PR, you are proposing that your client should increase their PR activity, so put this case and justify it with facts and figures which demonstrate the benefits. Then explain that there is more than one way in which they can use PR to improve their profile.

Briefly outline your possibilities, and then examine the pros and cons of each one:

- how it works or what it entails (half a day a fortnight spent generating four press releases a month, and following up previous press releases)

- what its benefits are to the customer (lowest cost form of PR, will increase press coverage and therefore awareness, and so on)
- what its disadvantages are, if any (without special events you just won't get as high a profile)
- what it costs (no, you're not giving a quote, but you can state that it will cost your time for half a day a week, plus basic mailing costs – whereas organising events entails all sorts of added costs of venue hire, catering and all the rest)
- any other relevant details (you'd provide the mailing list, the client would supply photographs to accompany press releases when needed, or whatever).

At this stage, don't express a preference. Describe all the possibilities equally and fairly for the reader.

Proposal

If you had a list of possibilities earlier in the proposal, you should run through them all briefly now and outline why they are, or aren't, the best option:

> **Solution 1:** half a day a fortnight. This is the cheapest option, but the financial constraints aren't tight enough to make this a significant factor. It will not generate such a high profile as the other options, and gives no scope for organising events, which are one of the best activities for raising both awareness and image simultaneously.
>
> **Solution 2:** . . . and so on

Make sure you don't pooh-pooh any of the options you reject, because some of your readers may have thought that was the best option. If you make it look like a ridiculous choice you are effectively criticising your reader's judgement. So explain why the option isn't ideal, but remain fair and objective about it.

This is your chance to express your preference from among the possibilities, if you have given a choice. If not, this is the largest part of your proposal and gives the information we discussed in the last section, minus the disadvantages. Either way, you should include:

■ Any facts and figures which support your case: the client's past experience, research findings, case studies, and anything else to back up your proposal. However, any lengthy tables or documents should be summarised briefly; don't bore your readers with the unabridged version. If you think they need it for reference, include it as an appendix.

■ Answers to any reservations you think your readers might have. You don't have to draw attention to the reservations, simply discuss the answer. For example, suppose you suspect that some of the board of directors might think that money spent on PR is a waste of time. You don't spell out this concern, but you can simply say: 'If the money is spent wisely, PR is an excellent investment. Research shows that companies who have a proactive PR function consistently score up to 50 per cent better in customer ratings tests than those which do not promote themselves actively.'

This section of the proposal should be perhaps a page or two long if you listed possibilities earlier, and between a page and about four or five pages if this is the only option you are proposing and you are therefore explaining it here for the first time.

When you reach the end of this section, you have finished your proposal, which may need summarising briefly. If the proposal section has been only a page long with no earlier possibilities outlined, you probably don't need a summary. But if this section has run to three or four pages, or the earlier 'possibilities' section did, you will need to add a concluding paragraph to round up the proposal, and acknowledge that the journey through the proposal has finished and we're all agreed on where we've arrived at. For example:

There are three possibilities for improving the profile of the company. Of these, the most cost-effective which still meets the objective of increasing attendance at trade shows, is to invest in half a day a week of dedicated PR activity. In this time, I can maintain a high level of coverage in the local and trade press, and I can also plan, organise and oversee three major events each year aimed at boosting awareness.

The power of persuasion

You need to harness all the skills of persuasion to convince your readers to agree with your assessment of the best way forward. A large part of persuading them, as we've already seen, is to show that you understand their business and the situation, and to give facts and figures to support your case.

But persuasion is also about psychology. People have to want to agree with you. And the best way to persuade them to do this is to start by agreeing with them. I compared a proposal to a journey earlier – a journey of exploration. Well, you're the guide. And in order to guide your readers through the journey, you have to start out from where they are, and gradually lead them to your proposed destination; don't stand at the far end of the journey shouting instructions to them.

Look at the situation from your readers' point of view, and show that you understand and support it. If you know that some of the people who have to approve your proposal before you can get the work are sceptical about the need for it, agree with them. You can say, for example: 'There is an argument that money spent on PR is often money wasted, because it has no directly measurable results. And it's true: sometimes it is wasted. This is one of the big problems with PR.' 'Aha!' think your readers, 'that's what I've always said. Here's someone who agrees with me at last.'

By agreeing with your readers you've persuaded them that you're someone who talks sense. Someone worth listening to. Someone they like, and want to agree with. That's half the battle won. You've put yourself in the same position as your readers and now you can take the role of trusted and respected guide. So guide them. Guide them through the argument to your side of it. You could say:

> There are several studies which show that good PR has a beneficial effect on a company's profile, but if you can't measure it you don't know if the result has been worth the cost. That's why I propose that we use a pre-agreed system which specifically measures whether the PR has succeeded or not.

Not only are you carefully leading the reader over to your side of the argument, you are also giving them an excuse to follow you. If they have always said 'PR is a waste of money; you can never tell if it's worked or not', they are in danger of losing face (or they feel they are) if they change their mind. But you've given them an opportunity to see your proposal as a logical extension of their traditional view, rather than as an opposite view. They can say 'You see; I was right. Here's an expert in PR saying what I've always said: PR is no good unless you can measure its results. So this is exactly what we need; a PR drive with measurable results.'

Presenting the proposal professionally

Everything about the way the proposal looks should give a smart and professional impression, and should help to make it more readable. This means that the language you use should be clear, intelligible and correctly spelt and punctuated. The following points are important to bear in mind:

- Make sure your spelling and punctuation are accurate: get someone to check them for you if spelling and punctuation are not your strong points. Don't rely on a computer spell-checker. They don't pick up misspellings which still spell out a real (but in this case wrong) word. So if you type *lose* instead of *loose* the spell-checker won't comment.
- Avoid jargon; that is to say, words which your readers will regard as jargon, even if to you they are everyday words.
- Use everyday, spoken English, not pompous words and phrases such as 'hereinafter'.
- Refer to the reader as 'you', and yourself as 'I', rather than using the third person.
- Keep sentences and paragraphs short.
- Use short words rather than long ones ('car' rather than 'transportation').
- Avoid clichés, and stock phrases such as 'meeting the customer's needs'.

The visual impact of the proposal is also important. It should look inviting, and encourage your client to read it. The most important thing is to keep it looking spacious, rather than cramming all the text onto the page:

- Use one-and-a-half or double line spacing.
- Leave comfortable margins, at the top and bottom of pages as well as at the side.
- Use plenty of headings and sub-headings. These break up the page, and they make it much easier for the reader to find information if they refer back to the proposal later.

- Keep your paragraphs fairly short – aim for them to be wider than they are deep.

- Use lists, either bullet-pointed or numbered, for information which can be presented this way.

- Keep the design simple: don't try to be clever with lots of different typefaces and fancy graphics. It just makes the page look confused and busy.

- Use appendices. These keep the length of the main proposal right down, which is a Good Thing. Summarise any lengthy chunks of information such as tables, charts, sets of figures and technical information, and refer the reader to the relevant appendix.

- Use simple charts and graphs to show statistical data. Often this is a good way to summarise information – a quick pie-chart in the main proposal showing where the marketing budget goes at present (25 per cent on printing costs, only 3 per cent on PR at present, and so on), and a cross-reference to the detailed figures in the appendix.

Adding the finishing touches

You have almost finished . . . almost. But there are just a few final touches of icing still to go on the cake. The following components all help to make a proposal thoroughly user-friendly and professional:

- Title page: put a cover page on your proposal which includes your name. For example PROPOSAL: 'To raise the positive profile of ABC Co Ltd cost-effectively, so that attendance at their trade show stands increases by at least 50 per cent. ROBIN SMITH.' Yes, you spotted it, it's your objective. Sometimes a proposal calls for a different title (my proposal for this book was, unsurprisingly, titled *Teach Yourself Freelancing*), but often your objective is the best title. It expresses the purpose of the proposal perfectly, and it is written in terms of the benefits for the client.

- Contents page: say what is in the proposal, certainly if it runs to more than about four or five pages, and include any appendices.

- Page numbers: it's difficult to write a contents page without these, but even if you only have three pages, you should still number them.

- Summary: Some readers just don't have time to read even a ten page proposal. Or they read it once, and then want to recap just before they go into the meeting where it's being discussed. So if your proposal runs to about five pages or more, include a summary right at the start (but you'll find it easiest to write it last). It must be brief or it fails in its intention. Summarise the three (or four) Ps in one sentence each, allowing a sentence each for the possibilities if you have included them.

- Glossary: you should avoid jargon, as we have already seen. But just occasionally a subject is so technical it is impossible to avoid it altogether. When this happens, you must add a glossary at the back, before any appendices.

- References: if you've used any research, interviews or reports to back up your case, add credibility to your proposal by listing your sources and references in an appendix.

All that remains to do now is to print out your proposal cleanly on to good quality paper. Put the finished document into a smart report binder which looks professional but not over the top, and which the client can remove it from easily to copy it. If you're in any doubt about its clarity, its ability to persuade or its presentation, get someone you trust to look at it for you and give an opinion.

Once you are satisfied, post it off to the client, sit back, and congratulate yourself. Writing proposals is not difficult, but it is hard work until you get used to it. After a while, you find you can follow the guidelines with ease every time.

Summary

- Not every freelance needs to write proposals, but a large proportion get most of their work this way.

- A proposal is a few pages of persuasive writing which will convince the reader that you are the best person for the job. It imparts the same information as having a sales conversation with a client, but it has advantages because it is in writing.

■ The first thing you need to do when drawing up a proposal is to identify a clear objective.

■ The information you need in order to prepare your proposal is information about the client, information about what you can offer and information to back up your case.

■ Structure your proposal according to the four Ps: position, problem, proposal and possibilities. And make sure that the proposal is presented professionally.

12 | GIVING A PRESENTATION

Another skill which many freelances need to acquire is how to give a presentation. If your clients are business people, this is often the way important contracts are won, especially if you are in competition for the work. This kind of presentation is not a big event with a huge audience, but a semi-formal structured meeting with a handful of senior managers or directors around the boardroom table.

A well-structured and delivered presentation gives your prospects the confidence in you which they need to spend their money on your services, as well as explaining clearly to them what you can offer. Like proposal writing, the techniques of giving a presentation are straightforward once you know them.

Presentations vs proposals

And in fact, proposals and presentations are much more similar than you might think: they are two sides of the same coin. Both are designed to inform the prospect of what you can do for them, and persuade them that they want you to do it. Both say – essentially – the same thing. What's more, they should say it in the same order. The only significant difference is in delivery; you deliver a proposal in writing and a presentation verbally.

There is one other small but important difference, and that is that presentations offer a kind of short cut compared with proposals. A proposal tends to be circulated to a number of managers or directors for discussion later, while a presentation gives you and the client the opportunity to get everyone together at once and talk to them all simultaneously. And this also allows them to ask you questions on the spot, which everyone hears the answer to. Of course a client can call you up, or call you in to their office, to ask you questions arising from a proposal, but if several people have read the proposal the odds are that your additional comments will be passed on via your main contact, and there is a danger of Chinese whispers. Your answers may not be passed on with quite the same emphasis or persuasiveness as you would have liked.

Since a presentation is delivered in person, it gives the audience a stronger impression of you than reading a proposal does. We all come across more clearly face to face than we do on paper. And we've seen before in this book that your personality is important, since hiring a freelance has as much to do with personal style and professional manner as with skills.

This fact, together with the advantage of getting everyone together and letting them ask questions, means that a presentation has the potential to be even more persuasive than a proposal. This is worth mentioning because often you have a choice between the two. If a prospect sounds promising you can often say to them 'Would you like me to put together a proposal for you?' Or you could say 'Why don't I come along and give you and your colleagues a short presentation about what I can do for you?'

My advice is to offer the presentation. The only proviso I would make is that a bad presentation has even more power to disillusion a client than a bad proposal. If you really feel your presentation skills are hopeless, but your proposals are very good, perhaps you should offer your clients proposals for the time being. However, read this chapter and practise your presentation skills, and aim to be opting for presentations within a few months.

Preparing your presentation

Your presentation will probably last about five to fifteen minutes, followed by an informal question and answer session. This is roughly the same length of time it would take you to read out a proposal, so you should include the same information in both.

The first stages

The first stages of preparation you need to go through for a presentation are the same ones we looked at for proposals in the last chapter (which you'll find on pages 131 to 139):

- setting your objective
- collecting the information: researching and then organising your material

■ structuring the presentation: the three (or four) Ps – Position, Problem, (Possibilities), Proposal.

Fleshing out the presentation

You will remember from Chapter 11 that when you put together a proposal there is a lot of information which you don't include in the main body of it, but which you put into an appendix instead. And there is information which you present in the form of charts or graphs because that makes it easier to understand. If you are presenting your information verbally, what are you supposed to do with all this stuff? The answer is that you either put it on paper and present it as a handout, or you turn it into a visual aid.

Handout materials

When we looked at proposals, we said that a lot of readers would rather have a shorter proposal, and don't want to be bored or confused with details such as tables of figures or complex technical information. On the other hand, some people *do* want this information. The solution with a proposal was to put the material into an appendix and refer to it in the main body of the text so the people who want it know it's there and can find it easily.

The same problem arises with presentations. Long or complicated data which isn't central to the points you are making can be summarised, and you can put the full version into an appendix. But when you give a presentation, it isn't called an appendix, it's called a handout. You still refer to it in the main body of the presentation, so those that want the information know you have provided it.

When should you distribute handouts? Do you give them out when you refer to them, or should you distribute them in advance? Or hand them out at the end of the presentation? The problem with giving them out before or during the presentation is that some of your audience may be tempted to leaf through their handouts when you'd rather they were listening to you. For this reason, it's better to give them out at the end – before you invite questions, in case any questions arise from them. You can put all the handouts together in a neat folder or report binder, and present them smartly. Bring along one for each person at the presentation, and a couple of extras in case someone else decides to attend at the last minute.

The only exception I would make is if you have a handout which you need to talk the audience through during the course of the presentation. Usually the relevant information can be turned into a visual aid for everyone to look at simultaneously, or you'll find that it can be summarised and the bulk of it handed out later. But sometimes you do have to hand it out as you speak.

For example, you might need to show your audience a picture of the desk space the computer you are proposing takes up, and the only picture you have which illustrates this is on the manufacturer's brochure. So instead of putting the brochure in with the other handouts, you distribute it at the relevant point in the presentation, saying: 'This particular equipment is ideal because it occupies little more space than a laptop would, but has much better picture quality – as you can see from the photograph on page three of the manufacturer's brochure.' Then give them a few moments to look at it before you continue talking, otherwise no one will listen to your next sentence or two.

There is one advantage proposals have over presentations which I didn't mention earlier: a proposal gets everything you have to say down in writing. This means it can be referred to again later, and there is no room for argument over what you actually proposed. But you can have the same benefit with a presentation if you want to. All you have to do is print out the text of your presentation and distribute it at the end as a handout. It will look just like a proposal.

As we'll see later, you won't read your presentation from a script; you'll use notes. But you will distil these notes from an initial script, and you can easily reproduce copies of this for your prospects to take away with them in case they want to remind themselves of any of the points you've made.

Visual aids

Some of the information in your proposal (in the last chapter) was presented visually, such as a pie chart or a graph, or a diagram explaining how a particular thing works, or a flow chart showing how a process is followed through the organisation. All this information needed to go in the main body of the proposal (sometimes backed up with more detailed figures in an appendix) because it was relevant to the main thrust of your argument. This information should go into your presentation in the same way.

If a point can best be illustrated with a graph showing the average learning curve of first-time computer users over the age of 50, you'd better have a graph to demonstrate it with. For a small presentation, which is what we're talking about, there are three main ways to do this:

■ OHP: an overhead projector is still, despite computerisation, a very popular piece of equipment. Assuming you have easy access to one (ask your prospects, if you're using their facilities) it is very straightforward to make up slides to use as visuals.

■ Computer: there are various ways to present visual information by computer, either on the VDU or on a larger projection screen. Check what facilities are available, and make sure that everyone will have an easy view of the screen. A laptop may not be ideal if some of your audience are sitting at a wide angle to the screen where the picture is impossible to see.

■ Prepared flip chart: prepare your visuals in advance and bind them together with a spiral binder on a portable desktop easel. You can simply flip on to the next page. This is a low-tec but very simple and effective approach.

One of the benefits of presentations over proposals is that you can use moving or 3D visual aids. You could show a brief video, or bring a sample or a working model to show your audience. If you're a designer or a painter you can bring an entire portfolio of your best work. So don't limit yourself to flat images.

There are good visuals and bad visuals. A good visual adds something to your presentation, a bad one doesn't and, at worst, diminishes it by being boring or confusing. You don't have to have any visuals unless there's a reason to. The following are the key guidelines for creating visual aids.

When to use visuals:

■ When a complex idea or process can be explained more clearly through the use of an illustration.

■ When detailed figures can be summarised simply, and taken in more easily by the audience, if you present them in the form of a graph or chart.

■ When you want the audience to remember one or two key points above all others. Design a simple visual, with plenty of impact, to make your point. For example, if you want your audience to grasp that your proposed computer system is so simple to use that even their high proportion of older personnel will understand it, you could prepare a slide or flip chart sheet with a cartoon or line drawing of a dinosaur sitting at a computer screen, looking relaxed and at ease, with the caption: 'So simple a dinosaur could use it'.

When not to use visuals:

- When they do not make your point either clearer or more memorable.
- When they are covered with words which you are about to say anyway.
- When the screen is too cluttered, or the words or pictures are too small, to be seen clearly by everyone in the room. Don't make the mistake of simply reproducing pictures out of books; these are usually confusing. Redraw them more simply and clearly.
- When the chart or illustration is too complicated to be understood easily. You can often split a complicated illustration into more than one; you could show the first phase only of a process as a flow chart and, once you've explained it, reveal the next phase and then the next.

Preparing to speak

Once you have written your presentation, and designed and organised any visuals and handouts you want to use, you need to do a little bit more preparation in order to deliver it as a spoken presentation.

Topping and tailing

When you had finished the bulk of your proposal, you completed the document by adding a title page, a contents, perhaps a glossary, and a few other garnishes to make it more user-friendly. You should do exactly the same thing with a presentation. You need to prepare a few opening words, and a closing line or two. Here's a run-down of what you should include:

- *Introduction*: Always begin by saying who you are and what you do, and thanking your audience for the opportunity to speak to them. For example: 'Good morning. I'm Sam Best, and I'm a freelance computer consultant and trainer. I'd like to start by thanking you for letting me come and talk to you today.'

■ *Route map*: If your audience were reading a proposal, they'd have a contents page to look at, and they'd be able to see how long the document was. But they aren't reading a proposal so they have no idea what's coming up. So tell them the contents and the running time. 'I'm going to spend the next twenty minutes talking to you about your computer system. First, we'll establish what system you have now, and what the problems with it are that you'd like to overcome. Then we'll look at the most promising new systems to suit your business. Finally, I'll explain my recommendation, and why I think it's the best choice for you.'

■ *Additional information*: You are in control of this presentation, and your audience is waiting for you to tell them the rules. The most common information to add concerns questions: when are they supposed to ask them? As you go along, or should they save them until the end? You often lose your thread a little if people keep interrupting, and even if you don't, other members of the audience can get rather confused. So the best approach is to ask for clarification during the presentation, but save questions until the end: 'If you don't understand anything during the presentation, please let me know and I'll do my best to explain it. But please save any other questions until the end, and then I can answer them fully.'

If the presentation contains a lot of material which might be confusing, or which your audience may disagree with (such as your assessment of the current position), you may want to stop for questions at the end of each section.

You may want to explain or clarify one or two other points at this stage as well. For example: 'I'll be handing out supplementary information, and a copy of the text of this presentation, at the end, so you don't need to make notes as we go along unless you want to.'

■ *Closing summary*: If you don't tell the audience when you've got to the end, they won't know. Obviously they'll work it out sooner or later from the silence, but it's much easier to tell them: 'So that's it. I think you'll find that the system I've recommended gives you everything you're looking for, and in particular that it fulfils your key requirements by being very simple to learn and easy to use. Thank you for listening. Does anyone have any questions?'

Putting your presentation into notes

If you're talking to five hundred people you can get away with reading from a script. But if you're talking to only five, or fewer, it sounds dreadfully stilted. So once you have written out what you want to say reduce it to note form, and put these notes onto cards. Giving presentation from notes, rather than out of your head, does not look less professional, as some people imagine. It looks as though you've taken the trouble to prepare for the presentation, and made sure that it will be clear and well structured.

Include subject headings and key points on your note cards. You might want to start a new card for each section of your presentation. You might also find it useful to colour code your key points. Write on only one side of each card, and always staple the cards together in the corner so they can possibly get out of order.

The only part of your presentation that you shouldn't give from notes is the introduction. Write this out (in spoken, not formal, English), and then memorise it. This will come across far better than having to refer to notes in order to tell your audience what your name is, and if you're at all nervous it will be easier for you to start with a few words you know by heart. If you are honestly frightened you'll forget your own name (and some people do get very nervous) put the introduction into notes as well but don't use them if you can possibly manage without.

Signposting

A proposal has headings and sub-headings so that readers can see the logical journey of the argument at a glance, and know where they have been and what's coming up next on the route. You need to provide the same kind of signposting for your presentation audience.

Tell them where they've been and where they are going. At the end of each section you should say, for instance: 'So now we've seen what the shortcomings of your present system are, and why you need to do something about it. Now let's look at what we can do about it. There are three ways we could go. First . . .'

Rehearsing

There's not much to say about rehearsing except do it. Lots of it. Rehearse on your own, rehearse in front of a mirror, rehearse in front of friends and family, rehearse until you can deliver your presentation upside down and in your sleep. This will show up any problems with it – your friends will tell you if any of it doesn't make sense, or sounds critical of your audience – and if you are at all nervous, rehearsal is the best antidote. Fear of presentations is fear of what might go wrong. And the less likely it is that something will go wrong, the more your fear will recede. With enough rehearsal, you will rule out most mishaps, and be able to cope well with those which are out of your control, such as the fire alarms being tested just as you're getting into your stride.

As well as rehearsing what you are going to say, you must also rehearse with any equipment or visual aids you plan to use. Otherwise you risk getting your OHP slides the wrong way up, or not realising that when you turn your computer on it will take you two or three minutes to get through the start menus and into the visuals that you want, so you need to have it set up before the audience arrives.

Giving your presentation

Once you've reached this stage, you've done most of the work, and you can't go that far wrong. But, as you know from watching other people give talks and presentations, some come across better than others. The most important thing is to remember why you're there: to persuade your audience that their best course of action is to give you the work you propose. Unless that work involves training their staff in presentation skills, they are more interested in what you have to say than in how you actually say it.

You should be less concerned with what you do during the presentation, and more concerned with what you *don't* do. As long as you don't confuse or bore the audience, prevent them from understanding what you are saying, or stop them listening with distracting mannerisms, you're doing OK. Anything you manage on top of that is a bonus. So aim high, but recognise that you can fall short of your target and still achieve your aim – of impressing your audience enough to earn the work you want from them.

Use of words

We've already looked at this in the last chapter on writing proposals, but it matters even more when you give a presentation, for two reasons:

- Stilted language sounds even more stilted when it is spoken than when it is written.
- In a presentation, your audience can't go back and re-read a sentence they couldn't quite follow the first time.

This is why you should not memorise or read from a script for a presentation. Write notes and then you'll find that the only way you can easily form the words around your notes is by using conversational English. As we saw in Chapter 11, you should:

- avoid jargon
- avoid clichés and stock phrases
- use short words
- use short sentences
- avoid pomposity
- address your audience as 'you'.

You should also avoid using catch phrases, such as 'you know what I mean' or 'the thing is . . .'. These phrases don't matter occasionally, but if they become repetitive it can start to distract the audience from what you're saying. When you rehearse in front of friends or family, ask them to tell you if there are words or phrases you tend to over-use.

Rhetorical questions

One very useful device (though, like anything else, you should be careful not to over-use it) is to ask a question and then answer it yourself. For example: 'How do you go about teaching three dozen people over the age of 50 to operate a computer, when none of them has ever used anything more hi-tech than an electric typewriter before?' This approach has two advantages:

- We looked at signposting a little while ago; this is a very good way of signposting what you're about to talk about, so the audience know where they are now, and where they're about to go.
- It creates interest, and gives the audience a reason to keep listening. You've hooked them, and now they want to know the answer.

Examples and analogies

Listening hard can be quite hard work, so you need to make it as easy as possible for your audience. One of the best ways to do this is to give them plenty of examples and analogies so they don't have to work out what you mean. So don't just say 'This range of computers is supplied with a full range of accessories': say '. . . a full range of accessories such as mouse mats, screen filters and footrests.'

Analogies often help to clarify difficult ideas, and you should always look for one you can use if you know you are trying to explain a new or involved concept to your audience. I used an analogy when I likened a proposal or presentation to a journey for which you are the guide, leading the reader or listener from their starting point to your chosen destination.

Delivery

This is the bit that most people find the most nerve-racking. But once you've learnt the techniques, it really isn't difficult. There are two aspects of the way you deliver your presentation to consider: your voice and your actions, or body language.

Your voice

The likelihood is that when you are not giving a presentation, your voice is relaxed and interesting to listen to. It is only when you begin to think – and worry – about it that the tension creeps in. So all you really want to do when you are presenting is avoid all the little characteristics that you avoid naturally the rest of the time:

- *Mumbling*: Make sure you keep the volume up when you speak, and annunciate clearly. It is essential that your audience hears you properly, or how will you persuade them that you are the best person for the job? Record yourself with a tape recorder or dictaphone and play it back, and ask friends to listen to you speak, to make sure you don't mumble. One particular bad habit to look out for is the tendency to swallow the ends of your sentences. Keep the energy and the volume going right through to the end of the last word.

- *Hesitating*: It doesn't sound too good if you keep pausing and saying 'Um . . .' and 'Er . . .'. There is a simple solution

to this: rehearse. Hesitation is due to lack of practice. If you
know what you want to say next, you don't need to hesitate.

■ *Gabbling*: The adrenalin during a presentation can cause you
to think you are speaking at a normal speed when you are, in
fact, racing through your words. Again, practice, especially
with a tape recorder or with someone listening, should show
up this tendency, but it will worsen during the presentation if
you aren't careful. So if you're a gabbler, when it comes to it,
speak as slowly as you can bring yourself to, and you should
be speaking at just the right speed.

Body language

As with your voice, you'll probably find that the important thing is to
avoid doing all the things you never normally do anyway. You want to
appear relaxed but not over-familiar: stand comfortably but don't sit on the
table. Try to avoid crossing everything – arms, legs, fingers. Aim for an
open, relaxed posture. But don't get so self-conscious about it that you
can't think of anything else. If you relax as you go along, your body
language will mirror the fact anyway.

■ *Hands*: if you feel really uncomfortable about what to do
with your hands, hold something with them – preferably
your notes. Once you relax you can put these down on the
table.

■ *Eye contact*: maintain eye contact with your audience – it
makes them feel involved and included. Make sure you look
at everyone, including the person over by the door who is
just sitting in for the first part of the session.

■ *Mannerisms*: as with catch phrases, repetitive mannerisms
can be distracting. So be aware of any tendency to keep
pushing your glasses back on to the bridge of your nose, or
fiddling with your rings, and do your best to control it.

Coping with nerves

Virtually everyone gets at least a little nervous before a presentation – after
all, it's important you do well. A modest dose of adrenalin running round
the system can be a good thing; it keeps you awake and on your toes. The
problem arises when the fear of going wrong or making a fool of yourself

reaches a level where it interferes with your comfort and your performance.

We've already seen that far and away the best cure for nerves is rehearsal. The more remote failure seems, the less you will worry about it. Just practise everything that you can, and especially the areas which you worry about most. You should also have – and rehearse – a contingency in case things go wrong.

Suppose all your visual aids are on the laptop you are bringing with you to the presentation. What if the computer crashes at the critical moment? What if there's a power cut? Be ready for it (especially if you're a computer consultant – you can't be seen to go to pieces over something you're supposed to be an expert at). Have a back-up: prepare a flip chart as well, just in case, and rehearse using it. Have a comment ready: 'Ah, I know exactly what's gone wrong (even if you haven't a clue), but it will take a while to sort it out. I won't waste your time; I'll just use the flip chart instead.'

Even with thorough rehearsal, many people still find they get very nervous at the start of a presentation. As it continues, they tend to relax, as the expected catastrophe fails to materialise. But a quick relaxation technique can help for those few moments before the presentation begins; a technique which doesn't involve alcohol – which never helps and can make things far worse.

The thing to get control of is your breathing, and everything else follows from there. When we are nervous we tend to take quick, shallow breaths. So make yourself take a few slow, deep breaths – the kind that make your stomach move in and out. If you can do it without being seen, a good yawn is an excellent relaxer. Every minute or two, just take one or two long slow breaths, and then go back to breathing normally. Immediately before you start to speak, take one long slow breath and let it out completely (under guise of checking your equipment or your notes). With the next breath, begin your introduction.

Dealing with questions

A small sales presentation is almost bound to stimulate at least a few questions from the audience, and you should encourage these. Only by answering them can you remove any doubts about giving you the work. In a small group like this, you are unlikely to get the kind of aggressive, heckling questions which a larger presentation can generate. Almost always, your audience will remain polite and interested in what you have to say.

Once you reach the question session at the end of your presentation you are actually into a standard sales dialogue, except that you have more than one prospect in the room with you. But you should handle the questions as you would in a sales meeting:

- answer any requests for information.
- respond to obvious challenges (such as 'Why is it so expensive?') without getting defensive. Ask the questioner to be specific if necessary, and answer the question honestly, remembering to give any compensating factors.
- Never bluff. If you don't know the answer say: 'That's an interesting question, and I don't know the answer to it. I'll find out for you.' Make a note so you don't forget, and remember to get back to them with the answer.

Once you have finished answering all your audience's questions, you should have covered everything you can to persuade your prospects to commission you to do the work. If your presentation is well planned, well structured, supported with visuals and handouts where they are useful, and well delivered, you have nothing to feel nervous about. Whatever happens, you will have convinced your audience that you are a first class professional.

Summary

- You may be required to give a presentation to clients. If your clients are business people this is often the way important contracts are won, especially if you are in competition for the work.
- The first stages of preparing for a presentation are the same as for drawing up a proposal, namely setting your objective, collecting information by research and then organising it, then structuring the presentation using the four Ps.
- Handout materials and visual aids are useful to provide back-up information and to illustrate points.
- Once you have prepared your presentation, together with the handouts and visual aids, you need to rehearse your delivery. Watch your body language and be prepared to deal with questions.

EPILOGUE

Some people never really settle to freelancing. Even with a skill to sell which people want to buy, they find some of the other techniques of freelancing, which are explained in this book, difficult to master. Others master them but never enjoy them, and for them freelancing just doesn't have the appeal they thought it would.

Many other people, however, find that freelancing gives them the freedom and autonomy that they want and can't find elsewhere. Freelancing is ideal for people who like to be their own boss, and for those who want to fit work around a family, another part-time job, or a time-consuming hobby.

I hope after reading this book you'll be able to work out whether freelancing will suit you before you commit yourself. And if you do go for it, I hope you'll have a lot of fun. The one thing you'll need which you can't get from a book is luck. I may not be able to tell you how to get it, but I can wish it to you. Good luck.

INDEX

Other related titles

TEACH YOURSELF

Marketing Your Small Business
Ros Jay

Teach Yourself Marketing Your Small Business is designed for people starting up or already involved in running a small business. Focusing on the type of marketing relevant to small businesses, it looks at

- brainstorming your market plan
- public relations
- corporate image
- advertising
- exhibitions
- direct mail
- selling and customer care
- keeping to a budget

A freelance business writer and editor, Ros Jay writes in a clear, jargon-free language, and includes checklists, practical exercises, easy-reference summaries and lists of 'Dos' and 'Don'ts' to give a comprehensive introduction to marketing a small business.

TEACH YOURSELF

Setting Up a Small Business

Vera Hughes and David Weller

This book is an invaluable guide to setting up and running your own small business. It helps you to identify your product or service and consider the marketing and financing required, and suggests where to go for further advice.

Starting your own business can be a daunting prospect. In addition to helping with the everyday aspects of running a small business, the authors give guidance on specialised areas such as legal requirements, self-assessment for income tax, opening a retail or office-based business, staff selection and marketing. 'Key facts' boxes in each chapter give a checklist of important points at each stage.

The authors have been running their own business for several years, and have an abundance of tips and useful information for the entrepreneur.

Other related titles

 TEACH YOURSELF

Book-keeping and Accounting for your Small Business

Mike Truman

This clear and practical book provides guidance on how to keep the books and prepare the accounts for your small business. Forget about debits and credits, journal entries, ledgers and day books – if you can read a bank statement this book will teach you how to prepare accounts for tax purposes and for the bank manager, how to make forecasts of your cashflow, and how to prepare a budget for your business.

With completely up-to-date information, the book follows the layout of the new Inland Revenue self-assessment tax return for preparing accounts. Step-by-step coverage of book-keeping and accounting makes this an accessible and invaluable guide for small business needs.

Mike Truman is a Chartered Accountant and a Fellow of the Chartered Institute of Taxation, as well as being a professional writer in accountancy and taxation.

TEACH YOURSELF

Time Management
Polly Bird

Do you want to maximise your time and minimise your clutter and chaos at work? *Teach Yourself Time Management* will show you how to do just that. This book explains how to record, monitor and improve your use of time. By showing you how to restructure your day and declutter your life, it helps you to cut down on stress, achieve your goals and free more time for personal needs. Managing your time effectively improves work performance and lets you take control of your life. This ultimate guide to getting organised, demystifies time management and puts you back in charge of your time and on top of your workload.

Practical, straightforward and easy-to-follow advice shows you how to:

- prioritise
- plan your own time
- reduce paperwork and handle phone call interruptions
- learn to say no
- delegate
- train staff to save time.

Polly Bird is a professional writer of business and training books.